ADVANCE PRAISE

"Chris possesses the rare ability to think strategically and implement tactically, which enables her to envision innovation and then carry it to completion. She has built her career on a commitment to organizational change through learning. As an advocate of realized human potential, she practices the higher-order thinking that motivates others to greatness."
— Gary Clemmons, Former President, GC Ink Co.

"Chris stands out as one of a handful of federal executives who demonstrate the excellence and commitment that can transform government."
— Jolie Bain Pillsbury, President, Sherbrooke Consulting Inc.

"Chris developed and led the single best focused and most effective leadership development program I have ever seen. Powered by experiential learning and storytelling in a framework driven from objective data, the NASA System Engineering Leadership Development Program took a generation of NASA technical leaders to the next level."
— Dr. Michael Ryschkewitsch, NASA Chief Engineer, Ret.

"I highly recommend Chris Williams as a keynote speaker. She draws on her creativity, insight, and vast experience with research, tools, and program design to tell leadership development stories that enlighten and inspire. What always stands out for me is her calm presence, clear communication, and ability to connect with any audience on the fly. She engages her audiences in a very genuine way that hits home with leaders looking to reach the next level."
— Ana Reyes, CEO, New Worlds Enterprise

"Christine Williams brings a tremendous gravitas and depth of knowledge to her work, making complex ideas available to anyone through her speaking and writing. She connects with her audience through her authentic approach, while bringing humor and fun to keep our attention and leave us wanting more."
—Lisa Saunders, Co-Founder & CEO, Arnie's Recon

"Chris's book came at an opportune time, as I was in a professional dilemma. (I wanted to end a long-term project to make space in my schedule for a new and more meaningful role.) I felt weighed down with SHOULDS, felt a good dose of guilt, fearing disappointing others, and resentment for being 'held back.' Certainly not an empowering position to make choices.

"In the first few chapters, it felt like Chris was inside my head as a trusted advisor and master coach urging me to take a closer look at my stories making up the proverbial wringer I was dragging myself through! Thanks to her kind and direct style, I used her activities to patiently create a deeper satisfaction as I reformulated my personal vision. Priceless!"
—Carol Courcy, Author of *Save Your Inner Tortoise*

"Christine's book is wonderfully written, filled with professional insights and personal experiences, and delivered with sensitivity and humor. She has changed the career trajectory of so many executives and senior managers, empowering them with the creative tools and language needed to effectively lead others and achieve their maximum goals."
—Victoria R. Thorne, Former Director, Career Management,
NASA Headquarters

"In this insightful work, Christine Williams has been able to zero in on the many doubts and fears that plague so many of us long after we should have outgrown them. The stories she uses to describe key fear scenarios helped me to connect with my own stories. I especially appreciate the way she ended with helpful tools that can lead us all to a positive ending."

—Ingrid Bens, Author of *Facilitating with Ease*

"Highly practical, wise, and impactful book with powerful exercises that will help every leader who wishes to move to the next stage do better. Highly recommend it!"

Magdalena Bak-Maier, Author of *Get Productive!*
and *The Get Productive Grid*

IF YOU DON'T ASK THE ANSWER IS ALWAYS NO

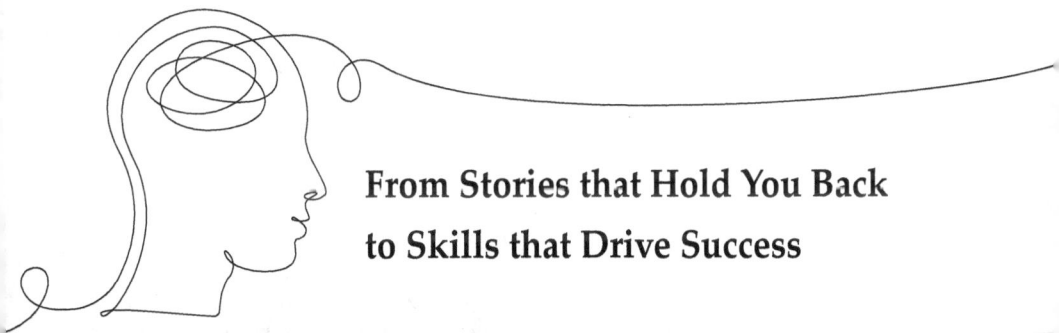

From Stories that Hold You Back to Skills that Drive Success

CHRISTINE R. WILLIAMS

Otto Williams Limited (OWL)

OWL Consulting

To request permission, contact
chris@christinerwilliams.com
+ christinerwilliams.com

Christine R. Williams
Otto Williams Ltd
OWL Consulting
P.O. Box 513
Crownsville, MD 21032

Printed and bound in the United States of America
ISBN: 978-0-578-30756-5
Library of Congress Control Number: 2022922992

To protect individual privacy, the names of the individuals in this book have been changed—with the exception of the stories which are my own and that refer to my husband, who has graciously given his permission. Some of the coaching situations depicted are an integration of stories that reflected the same or similar challenges. This was also done to maintain the privacy of these individuals.

All statements of facts and analysis are those of the author and do not reflect the official position or views of NASA or any other government agency. Nothing in the contents should be construed as asserting or implying US government authentication of information or Agency endorsement of the author's views.

CALL TO ACTION

All human beings live in story. And this is the starting place for success and happiness. Do we really believe we can get what we want in life or are other voices in our mind holding us back? We will start by looking at some of the most common stories that hold us back to help you see how these negative narratives are just stories and how you can change them to more powerful ones—stories that empower you and move you forward.

Once you eliminate what is holding you back, the next step is to lean into that forward momentum. Through my step-by-step process you will have the opportunity to define what is truly important to you and what will make you happy. You will also receive strategies and develop skills that not only put you on the right track but help you become skilled at asking for and getting the support you need from others to succeed.

I believe that within each of us is a spark just waiting to be released into the world to help us realize our greater selves, to build meaningful connections and to use our gifts in a positive way. Whether you are in an official leadership position or not, everyone has the capacity to influence and therefore lead a great many people through their example. I hope this book helps illuminate your spark and helps you light that spark in the people in your life. I wish you great success.

DEDICATION

To my husband Steve for his unending love, support, and belief in me.
To my parents Dan and Fee, whose love, sacrifice, and belief in education are the bedrock on which I stand every day.

ACKNOWLEDGMENTS

Thanks to my husband Steve for his encouragement, patience, and unending support throughout this journey and in every part of my life. To my fellow authors and friends, Lisa Saunders, Carol Courcy, and Magdalena Bak-Maier, who gave me timely advice, help, and the encouragement I needed to persevere through the rough spots. To my lifelong friend Denise Arnold-Lark, who never forgets me and whom I can always rely on for sage wisdom and a sympathetic ear. To my sister Karen Gross, whose early creative illustrations helped bring life to the visual image of this book. To my brother Bob Risotto, whose unique brand of comedy and wisdom has often helped inspire me.

I also want to acknowledge my two neuroscience mentors, Dr. Donalee Markus and Dr. David Rock. Their wisdom and research were the catalyst that allowed me to create more powerful learning tools. Tools that are helping many leaders and organizations reach new heights.

I had many good leaders who encouraged and supported me in my career and gave me challenges that both scared me and stretched me beyond what I thought was possible. In particular I want to mention Lewis Robinson (Naval Oceanographic Office), Stan Morse (NASA), and Dr. Mike Ryschkewitsch (NASA), three individuals who showed me by their everyday examples what great leadership really looks like.

Finally, to Bethany Kelly, who led me through the publishing process and gave me the guidance and framework to actually see my hard work beyond my own computer screen, Frank Steele, whose skilled editing was a true gift in helping me bring this book together, and Stefan Merour, whose design skills were invaluable.

CONTENTS

PREFACE

So many of us find that we constantly struggle to get what we want out of life. We begin to make progress in an area, and inevitably something happens to foil our plans.

Marie was a model branch head. She worked hard and set a good example for her staff. She always put in the extra effort needed for her organization to succeed. Many nights she was the last to leave, and when project deadlines approached, she was the first one in, often bringing coffee and muffins so her team could hit the ground running when they arrived. Her one fault was that she had trouble delegating and took on most of the more complicated work herself. She told herself it was just easier than having to train someone.

Everyone valued Marie's hard work and input, but when promotion time came, she found that she was passed over for someone less experienced. In our coaching session, Marie said several times that her boss "*should have noticed*" how hard she was working and the results she was achieving for the organization. I asked her if she ever told him about her efforts and their impact, and she said no, and repeated he "*should have noticed.*"

This is an all-too-common story. It starts with the false assumption that others think the way we think and value the same things we value. The human brain contains over 100 billion neurons that form about one quadrillion synapses that transmit information throughout our body. Our thinking, behavior, actions, ideas, and observations are all created and influenced by this vast neurological network. Since the likelihood of someone having exactly the same life experiences, producing the exact same thinking and making the same assumptions as us is probably zero, we should assume that others *should __not__ notice*.

This not only happens at work but in every aspect of our life. An event early in my marriage put me on the path to understanding this phenomenon and the need to open my mouth and ask for what I need. Steve and I had only been married a few months when we had our first big fight. I don't remember what the fight was about, but I do remember storming off and slamming the bedroom door behind me. I sat on the bed fuming, but after a few minutes I started to calm down and my thinking became clearer. At that point I started to replay the fight in my head. What he said, what I said, what he did, what I did. In a moment of incredible clarity, my brain replayed the point in the argument where I realized I had expected Steve to read my mind. Now, my husband is a very brilliant man, but mind reading is not one of his gifts. About ten minutes after my epiphany, Steve came into the room and asked if I was ever coming out and when we were going to get this settled. I just started to laugh because I realized I had compounded my mistake by not telling my husband right away that all was well and apologizing for not being clearer about my needs and concerns. Somehow, I expected him to read my mind again, this time through a closed door!

Not asking for the recognition, help, or support we need may cause many years of sleepless nights while we wait for others to read our mind. Asking for help can be especially difficult for leaders. Once someone reaches a leadership position, they are looked up to as being the person in the know. Magically overnight, they are now supposed to have all the answers and take on an almost superhuman ability to get everything done, all while making it look easy. Leaders often believe the myth that they can't show any weakness or ask for help or it may somehow tarnish their image.

As a leadership coach in government and the corporate world, I heard Marie's story dozens of times from both men and women. In my over thirty-five years at NASA I had the privilege of designing and leading some of the most prestigious and competitive agency-wide leadership development programs. That means I had the opportunity to coach some of the brightest people in the world, and almost all, at some level, also struggled with asking for what they needed. So, if this is a challenge for you, you are in good company.

I started my career as an oceanographer, which luckily got me to NASA in the first place. While I loved science, I found I liked working directly with people more than I did with data. Thanks to the opportunities I found at NASA and my manager's openness, I was able to move into business management and logistics, where I found myself leading people for the first time. I struggled as a leader because I saw terrific potential in my employees but did not know how to tap it. It was not enough that I believed in them; if they did not believe in themselves, nothing changed. To learn the science of people, I went back to school to study behavioral science and organizational development. This was just at the time when neuroscience was emerging and giving us insights and tools that helped us understand how the brain works and how we could use that knowledge to unlock human potential. With science again as my lever, I had the tools to help people open up to their own possibilities. *If You Don't Ask, the Answer Is Always No* is in many ways a thank-you and a tribute to the great former and current leaders at NASA. This book encompasses some of the most powerful tools I have found to help people realize their own potential and take charge of getting the support and resources they need to be more successful and achieve their goals.

If You Don't Ask, the Answer Is Always No is structured to take you on a journey of self-discovery to better understand what might be holding you back and providing you with the practical tools and skills to release those traps, get clear about what is really important to you, and ask for what you need from others to realize your goals. Yes, it will take effort to shift your mindset and practice to strengthen your abilities, but as you work through the process, you will get better with each step.

3

One of the things they don't explicitly tell when you become a leader is that your staff can only be at their very best when you are, and you are only at your best when you take time to understand your own thinking, barriers, and motivations. Experts say that the most important capability of a leader is self-awareness. That was why the first three parts of *If You Don't Ask, the Answer Is Always No* focus on helping you reflect and gain a better understanding of what you really want and what might be getting in your way. But this self-awareness is not just about knowing your strengths and weaknesses and how to work with them; it's about knowing yourself better at a deeper level. It's about understanding how the stories you tell yourself can trip you up, and how you can change the story to propel you into realizing your *true* goals and help others do the same.

One of the things I found difficult in finalizing this book was defining its category so people can search for it. I decided that even though leadership development may be an overused classification, it is the one that has the most relevance, as the knowledge in this book comes from my experience leading individuals and coaching and teaching leaders and executives. The techniques you will learn in this book have been taught to, and used successfully by, thousands of leaders in industry and government with enormous success.

The other categories I considered were psychology, personal development, neuroscience, and influence and relationships. While this isn't really a psychology book, you will find that you will gain understanding and insights into what is holding you back and how to shift your mindset in a way that better supports you achieving your goals. While it's not really a personal development book, you do get powerful tools and strategies to help you change your thinking so you can practice and build new skills. While it's not a neuroscience book, I provide the science behind how your brain works and why these approaches are effective. While it's not a book on influence and relationships, you do learn to frame your requests in a way that allows you to get what you need by also giving others what they need and helping them say yes!

If You Don't Ask, The Answer Is Always No

INTRODUCTION

Taking a brain-friendly approach

If You Don't Ask, the Answer Is Always No is part information and part workbook. My goal in structuring this book in this way was to provide a framework that is brain friendly and allows you to:

1. Focus on and obtain information;
2. Reflect on what you learn and gain new insights into how this information relates to you, and with this knowledge:
3. Apply and build skills you can retain, recall, and use when you need them.

As one of my reviewers noted, "This book is tightly written. There are no fillers or useless words to try to bulk it up, so I am left carried along by the narrative." This approach was very intentional, again to make it less taxing on your brain by getting to the point. That does not imply that this will be a quick read. If you take time to reflect and apply the exercises, you will get far more from this book and in the end be much more skilled at asking for and getting what you want.

What it's about

The Power of Story—As humans, the way we make meaning in our lives is by the stories we tell ourselves. Then, we behave or act in ways that are consistent with those stories. This book begins by explaining this phenomenon of story and its power over us by looking at eight of the most commonly told stories that seep into how we live and lead and that hold us back.

Traps—Once we get attached to a particular story, we can set traps for ourselves that hold us there. We will look at the traps of negative labeling and ascribing negative intent and how they keep us stuck and reinforce the stories we tell. We will learn how to release the self-set traps and gain power and control over them.

Values and Vision—Have you ever set a goal and achieved it only to find it did not give you the results you hoped for? That in that moment of achievement you realized you were not any more fulfilled or happier? If anything, the disappointment you felt made you less happy. Even when you got the degree, the job, the promotion, the house, the partner, the corner office, it just did not give you joy or excitement.

Often what we pursue in life has nothing to do with what we really want or need. We often get distracted by what others—our parents, peers, bosses, or society—say we "should" want. This book will take you through a process that helps you define your true values and vision and ensures that when you ask for something, it will have a much greater probability of giving you the results that will make a positive impact in your life, your career, and your organization.

Asking—Once you know what you really want, this book will take you through a process of making powerful requests to achieve them in a way that builds connection with others and makes the process a win-win.

Even if you just skim this book, you should have a much greater awareness when your old stories are coming up and a greater understanding of how they might be negatively impacting your results. That's a great start! The more you see the impact of your stories, the more you may want to return to this book to learn the tools and strategies that can help you. If you follow the process and take the time to reflect, do the exercises, and practice the tools, you will be on your way to getting what you need, improving your personal and professional relationships, and becoming a more effective leader.

STAGE 1

Story

"Human beings are curators. Each polishes his
or her own favored memories, arranging them
in order to create a narrative that pleases. Some
events are repaired and buffed for display; others
are deemed unworthy and cast aside, shelved
below ground in the overflowing storeroom of the
mind. There, with any luck, they are promptly
forgotten. The process is not dishonest: it is the
only way that people can live with themselves
and the weight of their experiences."

Kate Morton, The Clockmaker's Daughter

Stage 1: Story

CHAPTER 1

The Power of Story

To ask for what we need, we must first become conscious of the stories of our lives that are enabling or inhibiting us. All too often the prospect of asking for something gets hijacked by a story we tell ourselves about our worthiness. "I'm probably not ready for that promotion." "I don't have a college degree, so I can't qualify anyway." Or, we tell ourselves what others are thinking. "She'll just say no." "I know he doesn't want to, so why ask?"

The stories we tell ourselves most often are about who we are and what we believe we deserve, or don't deserve. These stories, more than others' opinions or data to the contrary, are probably the ones that have the greatest impact on us, because let's face it, we believe ourselves more than we believe anyone else. Julie Beck in her article on life's stories states that the material we use to make these stories of our life come out of life itself and our own imagination.[1] Often, it is a complex combination of the two.

In addition to the stories we tell ourselves, there are the stories others tell about us that we choose, consciously or unconsciously, to believe. Many of these stories we have carried around all our life. Sometimes we adopt a negative perspective of ourselves from just one unkind or thoughtless comment made by a friend, relative, or stranger.

"The trouble with you is that you're you."

Sharon Salzberg, the cofounder of the Insight Meditation Society, calls this negative internal voice her *"inner Lucy,"* from the *Peanuts* cartoon. In the cartoon, Lucy says to Charlie Brown, "The trouble with you is that you're you." Charlie says, "I don't know what I can do about that." Lucy's response is "I don't give advice; I just point out the problem." How many people in our lives have carelessly made an observation that affected us negatively even when they had the best intentions? We may not even remember our teacher saying "You're just not good at science," but for some reason at age twelve we abandoned our dream of becoming a doctor.

Sharon's solution is to invite our *inner Lucy in.* Give this voice a name of our choosing, provide them with a wardrobe, and ask them to stay for dinner so we can keep our eye on them. Chances are you will continue to hear the criticism, but by building your awareness that even though your "Lucy" may still be talking, you can choose whether to let that voice drive your feelings and actions or to ignore it.

In the book *Crucial Conversations*, the authors describe the path we take to action. While intuitively we might believe that after an event happens, we feel an emotion and then act on that emotion, there is actually a step between the event and our emotional reaction. This intermediate step before we feel emotion is the story we tell ourselves about what that event means. We add meaning to an event or to the things we see and hear because actions in themselves cannot generate emotion, and it is the emotion that drives how we respond.

See / hear (something happens) → tell a story → feel (a reaction) → act[2]

If someone grabs my arm quickly, I might have the emotion of fear or I might just have the emotion of surprise. Depending on my life experiences and the beliefs I have about others' intentions toward me, the story I tell myself and my ultimate reaction would be different. The situation surrounding the event would also play into the emotion I feel. If I was about to cross a crowded street and was not paying attention to traffic, someone grabbing my arm might generate the emotion of gratitude or relief, assuming that person was looking out for me. If I am walking down a dark street and someone comes up behind me and grabs my arm, then I might initially feel fear. The emotion generated would all be in the story I tell myself about the other person's intent. This all happens quite quickly in our brains, so it is difficult to discern what comes first.

"Stories provide our rationale for what is going on. They're our interpretations for the facts. They explain what we see and hear."[3] The good news is, because we tell a story before we feel and act, we can control this narrative. We can choose to tell a different story, one that empowers us and helps us achieve what we want and need.

If instead of "I'm probably not ready for that promotion," you told yourself, "I am as qualified as anyone else in the office," and if instead of "She'll just say no," you told yourself, "I know she wants to help me, so she will probably say yes," then you would be much more likely to ask for that promotion.

The question to ask yourself today is: Do these stories really reflect who you are, your beliefs, your values, or your sense of purpose? Or, have you taken in a story that is particularly critical? One that keeps you from asking for, and getting, what you want out of life?

Stage 1: Story

CHAPTER 2

The Stories We Tell

Through my observations, coaching, and surveys, I have uncovered eight of the most common reasons we do not ask for what we want, and the reasoning differs depending on the want. These reasons, or stories, direct our actions and our willingness to ask for what we need and want in our lives:

1. We are afraid of what others will think.
2. We get to be right, or make others wrong.
3. We don't really know what we want.
4. We are afraid that getting what we say we want may change our lives or our current stability.
5. We fear that if others know what we want, they will do something to sabotage our efforts, talk us out of it, try to control the direction, or tell us what to do.
6. We fear rejection. If they say no, we hear it as a rejection of us, not just a rejection of our request.
7. We are actually seeking reciprocity from someone; looking for a person to acknowledge they owe us for past favors or efforts.
8. We don't believe our efforts will make a difference.

Let's look into each of these stories to help demystify them and hopefully take away any power they hold over us.

Story 1

We are afraid of what others will think.

Yes, the high school freshman who wanted desperately to fit in is alive and well and still worrying about what others think. If we ask for help, will others think us incompetent? If we ask for support, will they think us weak? If we ask for information, will they think us dumb? If we ask for a promotion we know we deserve, will they think us pushy? If we ask for more than what everyone else is getting, even though we are working harder than everyone else, will they think us greedy or label us a troublemaker? Each of these negative labels has power over us. After all, don't we all want to be thought of in positive terms?

As humans, we have a profound need for belonging and acceptance. Unlike fish that swim away from their mothers as soon as they are born, humans must depend on others for their survival for many years after birth. The support and acceptance of others becomes an integral part of our well-being. In our early years, it is acceptance of family. Later we rely on the acceptance of friends, teachers, colleagues, bosses, and ultimately society. Because these connections provide us with a feeling of safety, they can significantly influence the decisions we make.

We probably all remember times as teenagers when we engaged in activities that we knew were wrong with our friends. Our need to be a part of that group, knowing we had our tribe to support and protect us, was a much stronger drive than facing the risk of being thought of as a coward and possibly being rejected by our group. As humans, we are designed to be in community with others and rely on mutual trust and work together against uncertainty.[4]

"For it is mutual trust, even more than mutual interests,
that holds human associations together."
H. L. Mencken

Building mutual trust has a lot to do with understanding others and their motives. We need to believe that we are accepted for who we are and that others in our "tribe," our "in-group," have our best interests at heart. If we say or do something that defies that trust, we can lose that connection. As a leader, losing the trust of others could harm our reputation and the respect needed to influence others and decisions.

We know that being thought of as incompetent, weak, dumb, pushy, or greedy can affect our perceived status in our community or organization and therefore how others act toward us. We risk rejection. The process of social rejection, or shunning as some religions refer to it, has been used as a form of punishment for those who do not adhere to the group's norms for hundreds, probably thousands of years, and has even been categorized as torture.[5]

> Wikipedia defines an in-group as a social group to which a person psychologically identifies as being a member. By contrast, an out-group is a social group with which an individual does not identify.[6]

The in-group/out-group bias is important because people tend to prefer and have an affinity for those who are most like them. This bias can be expressed as our sense of connection or kinship for others and affects how we treat them. If we are comfortable with certain individuals, we are likely to provide positive benefits to them in many ways either consciously or unconsciously[7] that contribute to the quality of their lives.

If you think of this need to care about what others think from an evolutionary perspective, it makes a lot of sense. In the wild, survival is much less likely if you have to go it alone. There was, and is, strength in numbers to fight off the harsh elements, to share the workload and to offer protection. Even today, long after many of the harsh realities of survival have been reduced in modern society, this social need is still alive and well in our DNA.

> "A meta-study covering more than 300,000 participants across all ages reveals that adults get a 50 percent boost in longevity if they have a solid social network."[8] Matthew Lieberman and Naomi Eisenberger, neuroscientists from UCLA, have discovered that the same brain regions that register physical pain are also more active when people experience social pain or rejection. And, interestingly, they also found that Tylenol alleviates both physical and social pains.

So, if you are holding back asking for what you want or need because you are afraid of what others may think, give yourself a break. There is nothing wrong with you. That fear is part of how you are wired as a human being.

Story 2

We get to be right, or make others wrong.

There are thousands of conversations we have in our head every day that are designed to justify our thinking and our behaviors. This makes sense once you acknowledge that if we never share these conversations outside our own cranium, then there is no one to disagree with us, provide alternative information, deliver a counterargument, or challenge the logic of our conclusions.

If we don't ask our neighbor to trim her bushes that are growing into our yard because we have decided that she is a selfish, rude creep and would never agree, then we don't ask. We also don't give her the opportunity to say yes and fix the problem that has been bothering us. Why? Maybe because a yes might prove that she isn't such a selfish, rude creep after all. In fact, we might find we have misjudged her all these years and that all the evidence we have piled up against her might have to be thrown out. That realization can affect how we perceive our ability to judge others and make us question our own competence. Not a good feeling. Surprisingly, there are many who would much rather not give their neighbor the opportunity to do the right thing and suffer with the unsightly bushes.

"Our educational system is rooted in the construct of right and wrong. We are rewarded for what are deemed to be correct answers with ensuing higher grades, which generally lead to more successful lives. Being right affirms and inflates our sense of self-worth."[9]

"The need to be right all the time is the biggest bar to new ideas."
Edward de Bono

"Would you rather be right or would you rather have a loving relationship with your daughter?" I asked my mother this question when she was struggling with an issue that arose between her and my sister. She thought for a few minutes and said, "Of course I would rather have a loving relationship with my daughter." A second later she said, "*But I'm right, right?*"

The need for validation, the need to be right, is vital to our well-being. The drive to be right advances our desire to get ahead, which in many cultures is a significant value.

In being right, we put ourselves out there as the expert and shoot down anyone who disagrees. Being right, as discussed above, comes from a need to avoid shame, humiliation, or a decrease in our perceived status. We work very hard to avoid these emotions, even when it harms us to do so. You just have to look at divorce rates to see how this plays out in competitive cultures.

My friend Caroline told me how her mother used to never ask for what she wanted and always made her guess. When she asked her mother to just tell her what she wanted, her response was, "Any good daughter should know what I want. I should not have to ask you." The implication being that if you were not able to read my mind, there was something wrong with you. Ha, I get to be right again!

Caroline experimented with different strategies to better understand what her mother wanted, but she would never get a straight answer. She would say things like "You should know" or "That's for you to decide." If Caroline got it wrong, it was her fault. If she got it right, there was no reward or word of praise. This makes sense when you realize that any praise, reward, or form of acknowledgment would mean that Caroline got it right, and since only one of them could be right, well, better to just say nothing.

We can't even acknowledge we are wrong, even when we are asked a direct question. Think of the interview question: "What is your greatest weakness?" Haven't we all been taught to turn this question around and answer with something that shows what a great employee or leader we are? Answers I get to this question are something like: "Well, I guess it would be that I am *too* conscientious. I just can't leave the office until I know everything is done." Or, "I am really a wizard at the computer, and everyone always asks for my help. I know it would be better to let them work some of this out themselves so they would learn it better, but I hate to say no."

Making people wrong might seem the same as getting to be right, but it involves different thinking. Getting to make others wrong also comes from a need to protect ourselves, but in this situation, we are not putting ourselves out there as the expert; we just shoot down anyone else whom we perceive may be trying to put their knowledge, experience, position, status, or anything else above us. This happens whether that is the other person's intention or not.

This is the classic devil's advocate. The person in the meeting who can shoot down every idea but never puts forth an alternative proposal. In point of fact, I have discovered that the devil's advocate often does have good ideas, maybe even a better one than those proposed, but they are too afraid to put themselves out there. Why? Because they believe that there is another person just like them waiting to shoot down any idea they propose. When we hold back, it is often because we lack the confidence to put ourselves in a position where we might be criticized or we lack the skill to deal with that criticism in a productive way and keep our ego intact.

Finding ways to communicate with confidence goes a long way toward getting out of this cycle, and we will look at some of these strategies later in the book.

Story 3

We don't really know what we want.

As someone who looked to "find myself" for a few decades, I know deciding exactly what you want or need, and then asking for it, can be hard. If you are like me, you don't want to make too many requests of others; when we ask for someone's help, we want it to be important and we want to be absolutely sure it is worth the "ask."

Even if we know what we want or need, we may not know what to request of others. Do we want an introduction? Do we want information? Do we want someone to mentor us? Do we want the opportunity to prove ourselves or want recognition for what we have already accomplished? Do we know what would be most valuable to request in this moment?

What often adds to our lack of clarity is that small voice in our head that may make us "ashamed of wanting, or think we shouldn't want, or something that strikes us as irrational to want. Pausing to ask yourself just what exactly you want—not what you think you should want or what others want for you—without judgment can often be a surprisingly emotional exercise, but it's an exercise by which I think we'd all be well served."[10]

Many times, the situations or barriers that are holding us back are not clear to us. Our brain only gives us subtle hints that something is wrong. We find ourselves unhappy, uncomfortable, unmotivated, exhausted, or angry with ourselves or others, but can't pinpoint exactly why we feel that way. We just want something different in our lives. This uncertainty holds us back from asking for help because we don't know what to ask for that will move us forward. This is exactly why we need others. The reason we ask others for help is that they may have the information, position, experience, insight, or understanding to help us achieve our goals. All of which is to say that sometimes we may not actually know what we need, and others may hold the key. This includes our employees. Everyone in our organizations has their own unique vantage point, and though they are not at our level in the organizational pecking order, they may still have the answer we are seeking.

While we all believe we are able to accurately discern our own thought processes, actions, abilities, and needs, our vision is often "obscured by the positive bias with which we unconsciously can't help viewing ourselves."[11] I once heard someone say that the only spot we can't see is the one we are standing on, because we are blocking our own view. This is why we need others to provide an additional perspective to what we believe we are seeing.

The most successful people I have worked with are fearless about asking others for what they need, and they are also not afraid to admit they don't know what to ask for. In these instances, they take the approach of describing the challenge or problem they are facing and asking for thoughts or suggestions on a way forward.

I often saw this with the system engineering (SE) executives I worked with at NASA. Even though these were some of the smartest people in the world in their subject area, they knew that they could not see every aspect of the project without the help of all the other experts who were able to see different parts of the mission more clearly. Only by asking for each team member's expertise could these SEs fit together the massive puzzle confronting them. These executives were not shy about asking for observations, information, and advice not only on technical issues but also on how they were leading the team. They were willing to take the hard hits they sometimes got because they knew it was an essential part of mission success.

"Your greatness is not what you have, it's what you give."
Unknown

These executives were not only willing to ask for help, they also knew it was important to share their experience and help others to continue the cycle of success. When asked to speak to a class or mentor an employee, they always made time in their schedules. And, this may be surprising, but most executives and leaders are honored to be asked. Successful people often have a strong desire to give back, and sharing their expertise is one way of achieving that goal.

It's scary approaching anyone when we know what to ask for, but it is especially challenging when we don't know what to ask for and we perceive the person to be above us. When you feel that pull to interact with someone who you would like to know better or who may be able to help you, I believe you should act on it. In these situations, just making an observation about something you admire in that person and asking them what advice they have for you to develop that same ability can lead to some great opportunities.

Knowing what you want, what will be of value in helping you achieve your goals, depends on knowing your core values and the vision you have of where you are going—two things you will have an opportunity to discover later in this book.

Story 4

We are afraid that getting what we say we want may change our lives or our current stability.

Hidden inside this concern is the basic fear of success. As much as we have dreams and desires, the devil we know always *feels* better than the devil we don't. The devil we know is our comfort zone. It is what we perceive as predictable, and "Predictability is a desired state, even if what is being predicted is negative—to the point of being disastrous, dangerous to the point of being life-threatening."[12]

Predictability is one of the key elements that influence human behavior. Prediction is a primary function of the brain and the foundation of intelligence. It is the "knowing" what comes next that has been essential in keeping humans alive for many generations.

Your brain is masterful at seeing patterns, filling in the blanks, and guessing what comes next. Our brain craves certainty, and when we get it, we are rewarded. "See, I *knew* that would happen!" Is it any wonder that even a small amount of uncertainty makes us uncomfortable? Our brain wants to see the whole picture and all its pieces.

We spend our lives working to create as much certainty as possible. As children, we work to get good grades in school so we will get into a good college or training program. We work hard in our studies so we will get a job. We get a job so we will have a place to live and be able to put food on the table. We buy insurance for everything from our lives to replacing our cell phones. All of these actions create gradual patterns that ensure more and more predictability, and when we reach a point where we are comfortable and feel secure, we are afraid to "jinx it."

My parents would live with the most annoying inconveniences for fear that making any change would make the situation even worse. The term "just jiggle it" became a term of art for the upstairs toilet bowl that always ran, and the fix was to jiggle the handle till the inside mechanisms aligned to stop the water from running.

"No matter how bad things are, you can always make them worse."
Randy Pausch

Almost always with tongue in cheek, "just jiggle it" was applied to every inconvenience, from a loose handle on the cupboard door to the starter on the car that just needed the wires "jiggled" to get going. My parents were not cheap or incapable of fixing things—just the opposite. My father had a wide range of carpentry, plumbing, and fabrication skills and my mother was an electrical engineer at a time when most women did not even go to college. They just believed that until something was *really* broken, which meant not working at all, that living with the situation was far safer than tempting fate and hastening a total breakdown. As an adult I swore whenever anything was loose or broken in my home I would have it fixed or replaced immediately and never suffer the endless inconvenience and "jiggling" that I endured as a child.

I had this lesson reinforced when the mechanism for closing my dishwasher became misaligned and we had to "fiddle" with it for the dishwasher to close properly. "Fiddle," a close first cousin to "jiggle," just requires a slightly different wrist action. For about a year, Steve and I struggled to close the dishwasher every time we ran it. When we decided to move, one of the first things the home inspection revealed was the dishwasher failing to close properly. Obviously, the inspector did not grow up in a family of jigglers or he could have gotten it to close. As a result, the new owners required us to replace the dishwasher as a condition of the sale. Steve and I suffered for months only to end up giving someone we didn't even know a new dishwasher? Lesson learned, again!

This may be a silly example, but it shows how the unknown affects our actions and how far we will go sometimes to maintain the stability of our current situation. The more we have acquired, whether it be material goods, relationships, career advancement, money, or any other situation or item that we think we value, the harder it is to risk their loss. I say "think we value" because often it is what society perceives as valuable and we are yet to consciously weigh in on the decision, but more about that later.

Story 5

We fear that if others know what we want, they will do something to sabotage our efforts, talk us out of it, try to control the direction, or tell us what to do.

This fear has to do with our need for autonomy, which is defined as "the ability to make choices according to one's free will. (Whether or not that will is free isn't relevant here—only that it feels free.)"[13] Think of how often people have gone to war and died to fight for their freedom.

Studies have suggested that our desire for freedom is hardwired and is a critical driver in our behavior. Consider how you feel when someone tells you what to do even if it is something you may enjoy or even want to do. If you are like me, you feel a twinge of resentment, even anger if you feel you are being directed to do something. If, however, the same person asks you to do the same thing or offers it as an option of what you might do, you feel free to say yes or no, and that sense of autonomy makes us feel much better about the decision and our relationship with the individual making the request.

Many of us experience stress when we perceive that we are losing control over our situation. Autonomy is linked to certainty, as we discussed above, because "when you sense a lack of control, you experience a lack of 'agency,'" an inability to influence outcomes.[14] Webster defines agency as the capacity, condition, or state of acting or exerting power. We yearn to have power over our own lives.

In 1986, David Snowdon initiated the now famous Nun Study of Aging and Alzheimer's Disease. Studying religious groups has many advantages because the relatively uniform backgrounds of the study participants mean fewer variations in lifestyle confound the data. Over the past three decades Snowdon and his colleagues have teased out a number of links between lifestyle and Alzheimer's, including the fact that the study participants who demonstrated "choiceful behavior" lived longer.[15]

A Taiwan study examined 1,380 staff members from 230 government-run community health centers. This study revealed that job autonomy has a number of positive work outcomes, including greater work satisfaction, and less intent to transfer and intentions to leave.[16]

> According to self-determination theory, autonomy is one of our three basic psychological needs, along with competence and relatedness. Self-determination theory defines autonomy as behaving with a sense of volition, endorsement, willingness, and choice; competence as mastering one's environment.[17] In other words, the ability to determine our own lives.

Never asking for what we want or need provides us with complete autonomy to make our own choices. It also makes it a lot harder to achieve anything, because we have to go it alone, do all the work, and make all the mistakes ourselves. It takes a lot longer and is a much harder road to travel.

I learned early on that autonomy was a key driver for me. Most of the time I was lucky that I had bosses who would set the goals and let me choose my own path on how to get there. However, there were two occasions when my bosses were more micromanaging types. They wanted to tell me how to do nearly every step of my job. I found that I often became resentful and began to compromise my own values by only doing exactly what they asked of me even though I knew there were other things I could do to make the job far more successful. There is a name for this behavior that I often heard from people in the same situation. It is called "malicious compliance."

Once I recognized this pattern in myself, I knew I had to find bosses who gave me creative freedom in order to do the best for myself, for them, and the organization. In interviews I would tell potential bosses, "I have the potential to be your best employee if given creative freedom or your worst employee if I am told how to do my job. What environment would you say best describes this position and our future relationship?"

We never have complete autonomy in life, but choosing how much autonomy we may be willing to give up to achieve our goals is still a choice and can often allow us greater options to get the help and support we need.

Story 6

We fear rejection. If they say no, we hear it as a rejection of us, not just a rejection of our request.

Why do we feel that when someone rejects our request, it is personal, and we start automatically listing all the reasons why we are undeserving or unlovable? We can interpret that "no" to mean they don't like us or don't care enough about us to help us. Or, it may just mean they are unavailable or lack the skill or knowledge to be of help. Unfortunately, most of the time we assume there is something wrong with us instead of with the request.

Rejection is a very strong emotion. As hunter-gatherers we lived in tribes, and our very existence was dependent upon others. In earlier eras, being rejected or ostracized from our tribe meant certain death.

> *"Just when our self-esteem is hurting most,*
> *we go and damage it even further."*
> Guy Winch

Studies have found that even a small amount of rejection will activate the same area of our brains as physical pain. Guy Winch noted that the greatest damage of rejection is usually self-inflicted. We don't just "lick our wounds but become intensely self-critical. We call ourselves names, lament our shortcomings, and feel disgusted with ourselves. In other words, just when our self-esteem is hurting most, we go and damage it even further."[18]

Because our ego and self-esteem are so attached to hearing "no" as a rejection of ourselves, many of us never ask for anything we are not sure to receive. How sad, when so many opportunities are lost.

If you had siblings, you probably remember times when your parents gave your brother or sister something, and you did not get what you wanted. Who of us did not internalize that as a sign that "You love them better than me"? Just as that high school freshman is alive and well and living in your DNA, so is that five-year-old who desperately wanted a pony, and when we didn't get it, we believed it was not because we lived in an apartment on the second floor, but because our parents didn't love us enough. And so, we internalized that response not as "No, a pony is not practical in an apartment" but as "You are not worthy of a pony."

Merriam-Webster's 11th Collegiate Dictionary has eight definitions for the word no when used as an adverb:

1. Used as a function word to express the negative of an alternative choice or possibility.
2. In no respect or degree—used in comparisons.
3. Not so—used to express negation, dissent, denial, or refusal.
4. Used with a following adjective to imply a meaning expressed by the opposite positive statement.
5. Used as a function word to emphasize a following negative or to introduce a more emphatic, explicit, or comprehensive statement.
6. Used as an interjection to express surprise, doubt, or incredulity.
7. Used in combination with a verb to form a compound adjective.
8. In negation.

In none of these does it say or imply that you are a bad person, unworthy, or disliked. That is just the story you made up.

The word "no" has deep roots in our childhood. Hearing no from our parents or others in authority, whether it was related to a request or to our behavior, usually evoked a feeling of shame or a sense of not being good enough. These feelings can easily get stirred up when we hear the trigger word "no," no matter the context.

Story 7

We are actually seeking reciprocity from someone; looking for a person to acknowledge they owe us for past favors or efforts.

"The norm of reciprocity requires that we repay in kind what another has done for us."[19] It is an expectation that others will return a favor. While this expectation differs depending on our cultural and societal norms, it is always related to the idea of mutual goodwill. For example, if I invite you to a dinner party at my home, I feel justified in expecting that you will invite me to a similar event at your home at some future date. If you take a colleague's late-night shift so they can attend their daughter's recital, you may feel they owe you and should take your late-night shift when you need a similar consideration. We often have these expectations even when we have not stated this "you will pay me back" condition. Do you recognize how we are relying on mind reading again?

> Positive reciprocity is when a positive action is responded to with another positive action. In many cases "this norm is so powerful, it allows the initial giver to ask for something in return for what was given rather than having to wait for a voluntary reciprocal act."[20]

My husband and I decided early on that when it came to our family, we would give without expecting anything in return. My mantra was "I don't expect anything, so I am never disappointed." Yeah, right! Of course, I am always disappointed when there's no acknowledgment or reciprocity. But setting this expectation for myself did help in that while I was initially let down, it helped me not to dwell on my disappointment for long.

As I said before, the expectation of reciprocity differs depending on cultural and social norms, but it also depends on the other person's understanding of the value of what we have given. So, when we spend all day running down information our colleague needs, which they thought we had on the top of our head, it is easy to see why they may not have offered to help when we believe they knew we were struggling on our project. Our colleague never saw the effort we expended on their behalf and we never told them. If we remembered that mind reading is not a skill we should expect in others or ourselves, we might have said, "Well, that was quite a bit more challenging than I expected. After four hours and six phone interviews, I finally have what I know is the correct answer to your question." Or, if we knew what it would take, we might have told them up front to be sure it was important enough to be worth the effort.

We tend to equate not having to ask for a favor and just having someone see our need and reciprocate in some way for things we have done for them as evidence that they care about us. And this feels really good. What we need to remember is that not noticing what we need and not reciprocating does not mean that they don't care. Their mental wiring is just not making the same connections our wiring is making. And without our giving them access to our thinking, they can do no better.

Economists have studied this area extensively, looking at the interaction between fair and selfish individuals, and have noted that one key to understanding why people behave the way they do has to do with the environment or conditions in a particular setting.[21] Whether someone reciprocates in kind or as the giver expected is based on any number of complex factors: the relationship of the individuals involved; the competitive or fair-minded nature of the individual; the expectations of the culture; the existence of rewards or punishment; the perceived intention of the giver, and other factors.

From a European or Anglo-American perspective, Victorian-era etiquette is a good example of how guidelines can lubricate the mechanism of social exchange. During this time, there were rules for making new friends, keeping up with old friends, and even cutting out morally dubious friends. But most importantly, knowing the rules helped one show respect for everyone else, including servants, acquaintances, nobility, and clergy.[22] While we look at some of the Victorian-era rules of etiquette now and think many of them ridiculous, they did help to establish shared norms and expectations so people did not accidentally offend each other.

Every culture has its own set of rules, and in our more multicultural, complex world, we need to rely more on sharing information, explaining, and requesting what we need. This complexity can make a leader's job even more difficult unless they, and the organization, are operating under a shared set of norms and guidelines. Understanding of, and alignment with, an organization's culture can make a tremendous impact on whether individuals can perform at their best.

The behaviors of the Victorian era were strongly aligned with the Golden Rule, "Do unto others as you would have them do unto you." I have found that the Platinum Rule works much better: "Treat others as they would like to be treated." Of course, this takes more work because we have to be clear about our needs and ask people for theirs.

Story 8

We don't believe our efforts will make a difference.

None of us like to expend energy when we know it will not make any difference. Research is now showing us how the brain calculates whether the effort we expend is worth the potential reward.

> *Cost-benefit decision-making depends on a binary decision to either accept or reject a choice based on the expected reward or the potential loss.*

I have found that this story tends to be popular with two types of people: highly intelligent individuals and people who have been through challenging situations and have become a bit jaded by past experiences that have not gone well. My experiences have shown me that intelligent people often are victims of the second situation as well. They just use data and statistics as their rationale rather than admitting they have been burned by past experiences. Admitting past defeats could only make intelligent people appear weak, so they look for solid facts to back up the opinion they've already made to preserve their self-esteem.

The highly intelligent are individuals who are used to thinking out ideas and options and believe they already have all the information they need. When a highly intelligent person who is trapped in this story is challenged on an idea, they will often dig up the data and facts to explain why they are right and you are wrong. Often when new information comes to light, they tend to not let it in, because they see the matter as already settled. New opinions or ideas that do not align with their existing conclusion are rejected.

When having dinner with my friend Avery and her sister Jillian one evening, I heard this story played out. In spite of having two master's degrees, Jillian was still working as a waitress. This evening her sister Avery was trying to convince her to apply for an opening in her company. As soon as Avery broached the subject, Jillian was armed to the teeth with all the data needed to thwart any point Avery could raise.

In a very calm and professional manner, Jillian explained the research she had done in her field and how she would have to start at a junior position that would not pay what she makes now as a waitress. She also enlightened us with exhaustive statistics on how many applications companies receive every year and the percentage of people who are actually selected. She even computed how long it would take her to get a decent amount of vacation time to travel. The fact that Jillian would have benefits such as paid health care, vacation time, and much greater promotion potential in the long run; that she had a much better education than others applying at the junior level, so had a much higher probability of being selected; and that she did not have enough money to travel now did not influence her decision one bit. The matter was already settled.

After dinner, Avery told me how Jillian was someone who had tried and failed a number of times. She could not get the job she wanted out of college, so she went for her master's degree. She still struggled to get in her field, and decided to go for a second master's. When that failed to give her an opening, she gave up trying. Now every opportunity people bring to her feels like a waste of time and just brings up bad memories of her past failures. This was not the first time Avery has heard Jillian's dissertation on the futility of job hunting. Avery had heard this well-rehearsed speech many times and she fully expected to hear it every time she brought up the subject, but she had not yet given up.

"We tell ourselves stories in order to live."
Joan Didion

People who admit to being jaded because of past experiences are more aware of the story they tell themselves, but the cause of the situation is usually other people, circumstances like the economy, or an organizational system with policies that are restrictive or impose requirements they do not possess. They feel they are powerless in their efforts to affect these larger, more powerful forces, and therefore choose not to bang their heads against the immovable wall placed there by organizations, society, or the gods of fate. In short, they have given up. We all need the reinforcement of occasional wins every now and then to keep us motivated and help move us forward.

This is not to discount systems that are stacked against certain segments of society. Indeed, in every society there are many conscious and unconscious biases and barriers built against certain populations. All the more reason to ask for help in navigating these environments.

Moving Forward by Facing Our Stories

Identifying the story that may be consciously or unconsciously holding us back is an important first step. Only when we realize what story is holding us back can we change it.

1. What's my story?

If you are truly being honest with yourself, which of the preceding stories are most likely holding you back from asking others for what you want and need? There may be more than one. Put a check in the box *Applies to me*. Now for those that apply to you, write the story you tell yourself in your own words in the box *How I describe this story*. Do not limit yourself to these eight common stories. You may have another story. If so, add it or them to the blank rows below.

Remember, we all have different experiences and thinking that make us unique. The important thing here is to get clarity about the story you are telling yourself so you recognize it when it comes up.

My Stories

Story	Applies to me	How I describe this story
1. I am afraid of what others will think.		

2. I get to be right or make others wrong.		
3. I don't really know what I want.		
4. I am afraid how getting what I say I want may change my life or my current stability.		
5. I fear that if others know what I want, they will do something to sabotage my efforts, talk me out of it, try to control the direction, or tell me what to do.		

6. I fear rejection. If they say no, I hear it as a rejection of me, not just a rejection of the request.		
7. I am actually seeking reciprocity from someone; looking for a person to acknowledge that they owe me for past favors or efforts.		
8. I don't believe my effort will actually make a difference.		

2. How might my story be holding me back?

Identify an area that you want to move forward on and the story that has been holding you back. Make this your story, so use first-person narrative: I, my, me, mine. Next to it, practice writing a new story—one that provides the positive momentum that will move you forward.

Example

Old Story	New Story
I am afraid of what my boss will think if I ask to be given the new assignment as team lead.	My boss knows I am a hard worker. I have completed all my assignments on time and I am just as qualified, and in some cases more qualified, to be team lead as anyone else in the office.

My Story

Old Story	New Story

3. Stories and feelings

Maybe you can't hear the stories you have been telling yourself. If not, try to sense the feeling you have when you stop yourself from asking for what you need. Is it defeat, sadness, frustration, dread, apprehension? Name the feeling or feelings. Putting a name to feelings takes the power away from them. It helps to put a boundary around something that may otherwise overwhelm us and therefore helps us to contain its power over us. If you can't yet identify the story, that's OK. Just let your subconscious work on it, and it will come. For now, just name the circumstances or environment that triggers the feeling.

Example

Feeling	Situation/Environment
Apprehension	Going to my in-laws for dinner
Dread	Delivering the monthly budget report

Now think about the story behind the situation or environment. This might be a good time to start working on asking others for help. Describe the circumstance you recall when feeling that emotion and ask others what they think your story might be.

Example

Feeling	Story
Apprehension	My in-laws don't think I am a good parent because they always make negative comments about our children's behavior.

With this story, it's no wonder you hold back asking your in-laws for help with watching the children. What feeling and story are holding you back from making a request?

My Story

Feeling	Story	Request You Are Not Making

Stage 1: Story

46

STAGE 2

Traps

"A trap is only a trap if you don't know about it.
If you know about it, it's a challenge."

China Miéville

Stage 2: Traps

CHAPTER 3

The Traps We Set and How to Release Them

A s I said before, we can choose to tell a different story, one that empowers us and helps us achieve what we want and need. This power emanates from the ability to catch ourselves telling the old disempowering story and to choose another narrative in that moment. This is a critical skill in launching you to your next stage.

Previously we discussed the path we take to action from the book *Crucial Conversations*. After something happens, we not only add meaning to that action, we also add motive as to why it happened. Because we are using our own brain's wiring to come up with this meaning, the tale we tell is uniquely our own interpretation. "Any set of facts can be used to tell an infinite number of stories."[23]

The stories we tell ourselves about others set up the relationship we have with them in our minds and in real life. This setup, and how we feel about others, often impacts the interactions we are willing to have and whether we choose to ask for help.

For example, I see a co-worker, Dan, down the hall, and as I approach him, he quickly turns into someone's office. Do I tell myself, "Dan was probably late and had a meeting with that person, so he didn't have time to acknowledge me"? Do I remind myself that Dan is very nearsighted and probably didn't recognize me without his glasses? Or, do I tell myself, "He must be mad at me and is avoiding me"? Something very simple happened here, and when we come up with a story that puts us at odds with someone, it impacts our willingness or ability to engage with that person. What if Dan had the information your team needed to be successful? Or, if he had a friend who could get you in to see the mayor so you could get that quote you need to complete your article? If you stick with your reactive story that Dan's actions mean he is mad at you and you never validate that story, those opportunities will probably be lost.

This reminds us that we have to tell ourselves a story before we feel a reaction, and that influences the actions we take.

Something happens → tell a story → feel a reaction → act
Crucial Conversations

Depending on the reason we decide Dan is angry with us, we will probably feel guilty, sad, or angry with him. And those emotions will determine how we act. If guilty or sad, we might avoid him. If angry, we might attack in some way. None of these actions will open the door to improving our relationship with Dan.

If the story I tell about Dan quickly going into a colleague's office is that he is rude or mad at me, then the next time I see him I may feel the urge not to make eye contact and say hello, or I might make a sarcastic remark in response to something he says. Because of my actions, Dan will probably feel I am the one who is rude or mad, and the circle of misunderstanding completes. Dan and I are now avoiding each other and both feeling fully justified in our feelings and actions.

There are a number of ways we trap ourselves in our negative stories. Two of the most common and insidious are negative labeling and ascribing negative or malicious intent.

CHAPTER 4

Trap 1: Negative Labeling

Negative labeling involves using descriptions that put ourselves or others in a bad light. She's "stupid," "selfish," "an egomaniac," "an idiot," etc. Labels are terms we use to categorize complex behavior. It is shorthand that we assume others in our culture will understand. The problem, according to linguist Benjamin Whorf, is that the words we use don't just describe what we see, they actually *determine* what we see. If I label Dan as rude, I look for behavior that justifies my label and I tend to overlook all the nice things he does. My filter for Dan is well fixed in my label.

There have been a number of studies that show when a teacher is told that a child is smart, even though the child was randomly selected for the study, that the child's performance increased more than other students. This is the classic self-fulfilling prophecy. The teacher anticipating that a student will do well creates the condition where the student does well. If a label of smart can impact a child's performance, so can the label of dumb. That is why it is so important to be aware of how we use labels and language. It is not an exaggeration to say that the labels others give us or that we give ourselves can set us up for life. And in turn, we can set up others.

Think about how someone's careless comment affected how you see yourself. When you were young, did someone call you clumsy or tell you that you were not good at drawing or history? Did you just forget it, or is it a constant filter that you use to judge yourself? I have a friend who is quite attractive. She never thought much about her nose until her sister thoughtlessly told her one day when she was fifteen that she had a hawk nose, whatever that is. That was thirty years ago, and to this day my friend told me her nose is the first thing she notices when she looks in the mirror every morning, trying to figure out how to apply her makeup so it will look less "hawklike."

I have coached a number of executives who have carried negative labels all their lives and never feel that they have conquered this weakness. Not surprisingly, many of these executives have become quite successful using the skills and abilities that they were told they were weak in. These individuals never see themselves as having conquered this weakness no matter what they do, because the story is always stronger than their reality until they realize it is just a story and they have the power to change it.

One of the executives I coached, Jenna, was told by her aunt that she was disorganized and lacked focus. She spent a lifetime trying to overcome this weakness. When I coached her, not surprisingly, she told me that she needed to work on getting organized around her new project. This was not the story I heard from her employees, who said they all admired how organized Jenna was and her ability to focus on critical details.

When we got together, I asked Jenna what she had done so far to organize the project, and she showed me several documents that included design specifications, schedules, workflow diagrams, budgeting data, resource requirements, etc. I asked her how long she had been assigned to this project, and she said six weeks. Normally this level of project definition and organization would have taken six months or more on a project this size. I asked Jenna if she had ever seen this level of project organization completed by a manager in only six weeks, and of course she had to admit she had not.

With just that awareness, Jenna began to see how she had been holding herself to a superhuman standard to overcome a weakness she had obviously conquered years ago, if indeed she ever had it. After we talked a while, Jenna told me the story of her aunt and started to laugh. She said, "You know, my aunt had obsessive-compulsive disorder (OCD), and no one ever lived up to her standards when it came to order and focus. Now that I think about it, she had that complaint about everyone in the family."

Armed with this new insight, Jenna was able to change her story about her organizational abilities. Jenna's old story would still surface—it's not easy to break the habit of a lifetime—but when it did, her strategy was to look at the data more objectively to see if there was actually anything more she needed to do. She also changed her narrative and began to tell herself that she was actually well organized and focused.

Not only did changing this story give Jenna added confidence in her organizational abilities, but by not obsessing over organization, she had more time to work on the strategic thinking and communication skills her boss was looking for her to improve. A year later, her boss told her that it was her improvement in these areas that made it possible for him to put her up for a promotion to the next level.

Labeling comes full circle

You may not be surprised that what you dislike about others is eerily similar to or the same as what you dislike about yourself. Imperfections we perceive in ourselves seem to get amplified in the most irritating ways when they are reflected back to us in the image, traits, or actions of others.

> *"If you hate a person, you hate something in him that is part of yourself. What isn't part of ourselves doesn't disturb us."*
> Hermann Hesse

"If someone pushes your buttons, it may be because they represent something that you despise or fear about yourself."[24] When you get angry, do you see insecurity, selfishness, judgment, or some other aspect that you have been struggling to hide both from yourself and from others?

This is not to say that there is an exact one-to-one relationship between what that person has done and you, only that there is something in what that person does that triggers a reflection of you. If you find yourself hating the woman in the grocery store who just spent five minutes berating the clerk for not putting her eggs on the top of the bag, it may be because her actions have awakened a feeling of shame in you because you know you have been impatient and critical when others have not met your standards.

The Universal Law of Reflection states that the outside world is only a mirror reflection of that which is already within us. This law has another aspect worth considering: sometimes the mirror can be a reflection of your polar opposite. "Such is the case where you are overly kind, and through your kindness, you continually attract people and situations that take advantage of your kindness. You may be attracting these people into your life so that you can see where your kindness is being motivated by your own guilt or the need to get people to like you. Being kind in all situations and circumstances is not always an honorable trait, for sometimes we are forgetting to value and appreciate ourselves."[25]

Seeing the relationship between our judgments of others and our judgments about ourselves can help us see these individuals in another light and create space for understanding, or at least patience, which allows us to more effectively interact with these people. Again, your goal is to connect and find ways to create a win-win.

Moving Forward to Catch Yourself Labeling

1. Labeling others

Labels are a habit. If you followed yourself around for a week, what labels would you hear yourself using? For the next week, try to consciously catch yourself when you use a negative label to describe the words, traits, and actions of others. Become aware of how many times each day you use this label and make a note of the circumstances under which that label tends to be triggered in you.

Since labels are a habit, they tend to be unconscious, so feel free to enlist the help of others to bring them to your attention. Caution: When someone tells you they notice your use of a label, don't defend yourself. Just say, "Thank you for catching that label." Remember, you asked for help, so don't make excuses or make others wrong when they honor your request.

Example

Negative Labels I Use on Others	When I Use This Label
Idiot	When driving and someone speeds by me.

Negative Labels I Use

Negative Labels I Use on Others	When I Use This Label

2. What might our labels be saying about us?

In considering our labels, it is worth reflecting on exactly what we might be learning about ourselves. Go back to the list of labels you identified in the first exercise and think about how they may be reflecting what you think about yourself.

Example

Negative Labels I Use on Others	Insights About Me
Idiot	I know I often speed when I am running late and feel like a jerk for putting myself in that position.

Insights About the Labels I Use

Negative Labels I Use on Others	Insights About Me

Release the Trap

Abandon Labels

So, what does it look like when we stop labeling? Say you are in a meeting and your colleague Henry has just arrived late again. The old you might have said out loud, or just to yourself: "Henry, you are always late. You think you are the only one whose time is valuable." If you said this out loud, you are probably in for a debate with Henry, because you attacked his status and he now feels the need to defend himself. Or, you risk his shutting down and not giving you his best contribution because he is embarrassed.

If you hold your frustration in and never address Henry's tardiness, your resentment for him will probably continue to build, and you are apt to act in ways that could hamper your relationship. With each reoccurrence of an irritating event, our ability to manage our frustration steadily decreases, which is why the people closest to us often frustrate us the most.[26]

> Suppressing our frustration, just like exerting self-control on any of our emotions, uses up our mental and emotional energy and leaves us more vulnerable to making poor choices.

Ignoring the situation will not make it go away. There are many reasons why you may want to avoid a confrontation in the moment, particularly when others are present. But before you decide not to take action, be sure you are doing it for a good reason.

In dealing with these situations, pause and:

- Remember that this person is more than their habits and actions. We all want to be thought of as better than our worst day.

- Look beyond the specific incident that is bothering you and consider the whole person. Are there times when you have experienced this person in a more positive light?
- And remember, we all make mistakes. We are all human. I know this is not easy, particularly when someone's behavior is frustrating or is having a negative impact on the team, but it is always worth a try.

Instead, use neutral (descriptive) language.

Neutral language is a way of describing events, behaviors, and actions that eliminates or greatly reduces the negative emotional baggage either for us or for the person with whom we are dealing.

Saying "You started speaking before I finished my thought" provides far more clarity than "You were rude and disrespectful." It also leaves the door open to working toward a solution instead of the other person shutting down or attacking in return.

Learning to use neutral language can be a bit tricky at first, and you may have to rework your stories a couple of times to get all the negative connotations out of them. Let's look at a few examples:

Label	What They Actually Did
Idiot	They were not paying attention and bumped into you.

Slob	She did not hang up her coat.
The B* Word	Publicly disparaged your report after you asked them for feedback before you presented it.

Labeling or negative name-calling is actually verbal abuse. For those of us who find any kind of abuse abhorrent and still find ourselves labeling people, this is a difficult but important realization.

Name-calling or labeling is a disease that infects us all.[27] There are many reasons why we do it: habit, to feel better/superior, to retaliate, to release our frustrations, even sometimes just for fun. Our favorite or most used insults may even be cultural.

Researchers sampled 3,000 people, asking how they might respond to someone rudely bumping into them, and found that the pungent expressions generated varied depending on their nationality. How we disparage others reveals who we are and what we value.[28]

Whatever the reason, or our particular preferred labels, it is worth becoming aware of them and knowing when to make another choice.

Okay, since we can't be good all the time, I'll give you special dispensation when you are alone to yell at other drivers that cut you off or at the TV or the radio when someone says something outrageous, as long as they can't hear you.

You might be asking; "So why are we talking about negative labeling when what I want to do is ask people for help?" Fair question. The reason is that these habits can keep us trapped in our old stories and provide convenient excuses as to why we don't ask for what we need.

Often what you need to move your goals forward is not for someone to do something more, but for something to stop. You want your partner to stop interrupting you; you want your colleague to stop coming to the meeting late; you want your brother-in-law to not criticize your driving. Learning to use neutral language is a critical skill when addressing behaviors and asking for what you need, so we will be looking into this more with another tool.

Moving Forward to Abandon Labels

1. Notice and reframe

Over the next week, notice the stories you tell about others and yourself and the labels you use. Write what you would usually think or say and then try to see if you can reframe this situation in neutral language.

Example

Name	Label	Current Story	Neutral Story
Henry	Arrogant	He thinks his time is more important than the rest of us.	Henry arrived ten minutes after the start of the meeting.
Me	Stupid	I am so bad at math.	I did not add this column of numbers correctly.

Your stories

Name	Label	Current Story	Neutral Story

CHAPTER 5

Trap 2: Ascribing Negative Intent

A scribing negative or malicious intent means we believe the motives behind the actions taken by others are intended to harm us. We just *know* when Dan "ducked" into an office that he did it to avoid us. We *know* that when we get interrupted in a meeting that the intent was to shut us down because we disagreed with someone more senior. We *are sure* the reason our friend did not return our call is that they are angry with us for canceling our dinner plans. Again, we are resorting to mind reading, but this time we are the ones attempting to read other people's minds.

"If you walk in with fear and anger, you will find fear and anger."
John-Roger Hinkins

One of my clients, Linda, told me about convening a teleconference with her team and a potential new customer. She sent out an agenda a week beforehand, included a detailed summary of the project schedule describing critical issues that needed to be discussed, and ensured the right people were invited who had knowledge of each aspect of the project.

Linda said the client joined the call ten minutes late and proceeded to take over the meeting. He rambled on, got into issues that were not relevant, and cut her off each time she tried to intervene. At some point she just gave up trying. Needless to say, the meeting was a disaster. None of the objectives were achieved, the project team members were now frustrated and confused, and Linda spent most of the following two days doing damage control. Linda was a successful female executive who was the first woman in many of the positions she held, so this type of domineering behavior was not new to her. When she told me the story, she said she was sure the reason her client behaved this way was that he did not want a woman leading his project and was probably challenging her authority to get a man assigned instead.

While Linda might have been shut down in that moment, she was not one to accept defeat. As we talked, Linda began to see the reasons she imputed to her client's motivations were just a story, and she decided to set up a face-to-face meeting with the client to discuss her concerns about how his actions made it hard for her to achieve the meeting goals. After she recounted the planning and objectives for the meeting and what actually happened, she said her client became very quiet and visibly upset.

As it turned out, his distress was not with her, but with himself. Her client said he had not received the pre-material or agenda she sent because of an internal email problem the week before. As he had not seen a formal structure or agenda, he assumed his role in the meeting was just to brainstorm his thoughts and ideas with the team.

Her client also said he was somewhat of an extrovert and had often been accused of cutting people off and had been working on that, but telecoms were still a particular challenge for him because of audio delays and not being able to see people's feedback. The client went on to tell Linda that in fact he was thrilled to be working with a woman of her experience and knowledge and asked her to be sure to provide feedback on what he could do better to support the project in the future.

In ascribing nefarious or malicious intent, we assume the other person means us harm or at least does not have our best interest at heart. That is because when we feel offended, we can quickly shift into a threat state and do not think about other reasons why this might be happening. We feel the compelling urge to move into a position where we can protect ourselves, and usually that involves retreating or attacking.

"Fully 95 percent of our behavior, feeling, and response is habitual."
Maxwell Maltz

Personal expression is a habit, and this habit developed because it has probably worked well for us in the past. If it hasn't worked well, we may not have been given that feedback or may not know what to do instead. In this case, the client used his well-developed, extroverted energy to jump into the meeting and start throwing out ideas before he learned what was going on. In Linda's case, when things did not go as planned, she shut down, which she admitted was her habit whenever she felt threatened or disrespected. Linda rationalized this habitual response because she told herself it was better than creating a problem with her client.

When I asked Linda where she thought that response came from, she told me that her family was very conflict-averse. Differences of opinion were seen as potentially causing rifts in the extended family, so she and her mother became masters at either changing the subject or just not responding at all. Before family get-togethers, Linda and her mother would plan topics to introduce to hopefully keep more contentious topics from emerging.

Because our habitual behaviors travel a well-worn path, we can always come up with great rationale for our behavior. Many of the scripts for these stories are well rehearsed and often involve blaming others either for what they did or didn't do, or for what we imagined they were thinking or assumed they would do next. Our reactions are always very well aligned with our rationale. Unfortunately, we do not always take the time to test our hypotheses and assumptions.

Moving Forward to Catch Myself Ascribing Negative Intent

1. Relationships

Ascribing negative intent has much to do with the relationship we have with people. If we trust someone and know they have our best interest at heart, we can take criticism and overlook certain actions. This exercise is similar to the one above to catch yourself in the act, but this time you are looking for moments when you are making negative assumptions about people or situations without all the data. Do you really know what's going on? Be honest with yourself. Are you feeling threatened or being self-defensive? When you are being defensive, your perspective narrows and you stop listening and are likely to be missing important information.

In this exercise think about the relationship you have with the person involved. How well do you know this person and how would you rate your current relationship?

Example:

Who? How well I know them (quality of relationship)	What? What was the situation and what did they do?	Story? What intent did I ascribe?
Neighbor Don't know her at all	Grass has not been cut in weeks.	She is lazy and does not care about the image of the neighborhood.

Who? How well I know them (quality of relationship)	What? What was the situation and what did they do?	Story? What intent did I ascribe?

2. What might ascribing negative intent say about me?

Consider the motives you are ascribing to others.

Example:

Negative Intent I Ascribed	Insights About Me
She is lazy and does not care about the image of the neighborhood.	I feel all my hard work on making my home look good is wasted, because no matter what I do, that eyesore is right next door, and I feel helpless to do anything about it.

Negative Intent I Ascribed	Insights About Me

Release the Trap

Assume Positive Intent

In assuming positive intent, we start with the belief that the sender of the message or initiator of the action means only the best for us. We further assume that they may not have all the facts or that they may not know how to express themselves in a way that works for us. "It means when we are presented with a situation in which we might feel attacked or criticized, we have to take a step back and look at it from a new angle. It also means that what feels like a very real threat may be someone actually trying to help us grow and be more successful—to believe that the person speaking has no hidden agenda."[29]

Instead of immediately going into defensive mode and letting ourselves be offended, we should pause and ask why someone might be acting in this way. When we pause, we give ourselves the critical few seconds we need to disrupt our reptile brain and question our own rationale and conclusions. And, just as we had hoped for them, choose another more useful response. One of the most successful ways I have found to short-circuit the defensive response is to ask a question that starts with "I wonder why." I wonder why he just said that? I wonder why she walked away so abruptly? I wonder why he is looking at me that way? I wonder why she keeps interrupting me?

We sometimes find ourselves getting uncomfortable or angry toward someone or something but can't quite put our finger on why we are feeling that way. These are times when our intuitive sense tells us something is off, but in the moment, we are not able to know what the threat is, only that we feel one. In these situations, I turn the question on myself. *I wonder why* I am feeling threatened, or uncomfortable, or starting to get angry? Again, using a question like "I wonder why" gives us the opportunity to slow down our threat response and focus on problem solving rather than reacting.

"I wonder why ..."

I had a client, Jamila, who told me about a situation she had with one of her employees. James tended to monopolize meetings. He would start giving input on an issue and would tell long, sometimes seemingly irrelevant stories to make his points. Once he started talking, people in the meeting would roll their eyes, take out their phones, and stop paying attention. The more Jamila would try to cut him off or move on, the more he seemed to interject, and when asked to let others talk, he would sulk and say he was hurt because everyone else got to speak but he was being cut off. Jamila even paid for James to take a communications course, but his skills did not improve.

Jamila said she had tried every facilitation strategy in the book and still was unable to get him to change his behavior. When those strategies did not work, she was ashamed to say she too started taking out her phone, hoping he would get the hint. That only seemed to make it worse.

Her other employees were complaining and some even threatened to stop coming to meetings. She spoke to James privately about talking too much in meetings, but all he said was that his input was important to the issue and how else was he to share it? She suggested using an email, but he complained that it was too complex to explain in an email. Jamila knew James was quite intelligent, but she was so frustrated with his inability to get to the point that she began to give him only minor assignments, hoping he would not have much to say in meetings. That did not work either.

Jamila was at the end of her rope, until one meeting while James started speaking, she decided to stop thinking about why James needed to talk so much and begin focusing on her reaction. She then asked herself, "I wonder why I am reacting this way when James speaks?"

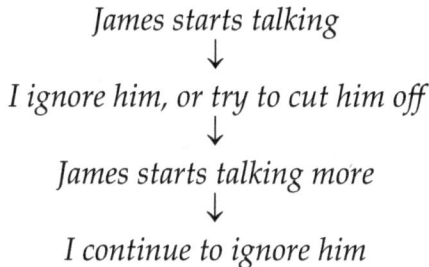

James starts talking
↓
I ignore him, or try to cut him off
↓
James starts talking more
↓
I continue to ignore him

When Jamila had a moment to consider the question "I wonder why I am reacting like this?" she realized that it was not just James she was upset with, but herself. She admitted she was not a patient person, and because she was so busy, she resented the time James took to explain things during meetings. She realized by ignoring him and taking out her phone she was unconsciously trying to punish him for taking up so much of her time.

When she became aware that her own behavior might be contributing to James continuing to talk so much, she decided to try a different approach. Instead of looking down or taking out her phone when James spoke, she made an extra effort to listen. She made sure to make eye contact with him, nodded to let him know she was listening, and took a few notes on what he said. Within five minutes she felt she had a good grasp of the points he was trying to make and asked him if she could interrupt him for a second to ensure she understood the issue. She then referred to her notes, summarized James's two key points, and asked him, "Do I have this right?" He said "Yes." She then asked if there was anything he wanted to add, and he said "No." At that point the meeting was able to proceed.

James starts talking
↓
I assume positive intent and pay attention
↓
James now knows he has been heard and no longer needs to keep talking
↓
I no longer feel negative about James

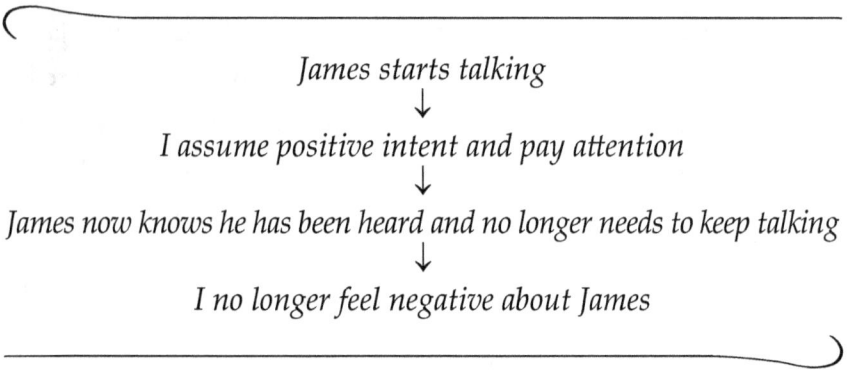

It is not uncommon to lose sight of how we may be contributing to a situation by our words and actions. We intend one thing but our actions or words end up having the opposite effect. Being reflective and seeing how we have misunderstood past situations can help us to be more open and inquisitive when we begin to feel frustrated, offended, or angered by the words or actions of others. When we opt to give others the benefit of the doubt and respond without judgment, we also give ourselves the space to find hidden opportunities in what could otherwise be a bad situation.

"Assigning negative intent essentially 'calls into question our cherished beliefs about our own human decency.'"[30]
Miki Kashtan, PhD

Changing the script

In writing my story about James, I remembered another story where the challenge to change the situation and get what we really needed seemed insurmountable. The situation was an extended family holiday get-together. What Gwen wanted was for everyone to get along and to have a peaceful and enjoyable visit together.

As it turns out, "catastrophe" is often a universal synonym for a holiday get-together. A number of people I know have their own version of the *Holiday Horror*

Show. What they all had in common was that each year the drama, the fights, the bad behavior, the insults, the crying, and the hurt feelings were almost exactly the same as they were the year before, … and the year before that, … and the year before that, … and, well, you get the picture. And yet, every year they all trudged back into the lions' den, hoping desperately for things to be different. We tell ourselves, *THIS* year it will be different.

Let's be honest. Norman Rockwell's happy images and Hallmark's joyful messages can create an expectation that is quite challenging to achieve. If we could see how our habits influence our holiday gatherings, maybe we could better prepare for them. If you are one of the lucky ones who have great holiday gatherings and this example below does not resonate with you, count your blessings and try to apply the concept to a situation where you have a script that could be holding you back.

Dear Family and Friends,

Please join us for another hopeless attempt to put our differences aside and get along for one day a year.

In keeping with this year's theme: Different Year, Same Script

Our menu will feature lots of your traditional favorites:

- *Down in the Dumps Deviled Eggs*
- *Melancholy Meats*
- *Resentful Roast*
- *Sarcastic Soup*
- *Pitiful Potatoes, and*
- *Pessimistic Pumpkin Pie*

As always, large amounts of the three a's— alcohol, aspirin, and antacid—will be on hand.

We do not look forward to seeing you, but come anyway, and please RSVP late, as usual.

While it is often helpful to add humor to situations, I don't recommend this type of tongue-in-cheek invitation as it increases the risk of escalating the conflict inherent in these *festivities*. Believe me, no matter how clever you think you are, someone will be offended.

Some people describe their holiday get-together as a disaster movie or impending hurricane. The gathering starts with one or two people tossing around a few thoughtless comments. Soon everyone joins in, until the action reaches a noisy and shattering climax, after which some people storm out while others retreat into safe corners until they can come up with a good excuse why they need to leave early.

Others describe their holiday get-together as a series of sorties, or more like a set of one-act plays, with small groups coming together, speaking their lines, getting hurt or mad, and then people moving on to the next grouping, where the players and topics shift but the dynamics and results are the same, with lots of conflict and bruised relationships. There is, of course, a better way to face these potentially toxic social gatherings, and that is to change the theme from *Different Year, Same Script* to *Different Year, Different Script*.

Gwen found this solution one year when, as always, her house was bursting at the seams with relatives. This included overtired adults who were cranky from the long drive with their restless children singing that beloved holiday classic "Are we there yet?" every five minutes for the last two hundred miles. A washer and too few bathrooms were operating overtime trying to get everyone clean, dressed, and ready before the in-town guests were scheduled to arrive. And, this year had the added excitement of an inquisitive five-year-old whose love of turning knobs and whose curiosity shut off the oven for an hour put the turkey far behind the seven other perfectly timed gourmet dishes.

As time got closer, Gwen's tension increased because she knew her brother was going to belittle her efforts, as he always did. As her brother pulled up the driveway, Gwen said she started to feel the tension in her stomach, and this was when the curtain usually went up on the play Gwen called *Holiday Tragedy: The Arrival*.

Ed: "*HELLO!!!*" (Storming through the front door announcing his arrival in his familiar booming voice. Then before anyone can answer, he continues.) "Well, sis, you did it again. You timed dinner perfectly so I would hit the maximum amount of traffic crossing the bridge. Don't know why you can't schedule dinner an hour later to avoid the noon rush."

With this familiar opening cue, Gwen felt herself pick up her well-rehearsed script and started playing her part.

Gwen (in the most cynical voice she could muster): "Oh, you poor thing, did you spend an extra fifteen minutes in traffic? How thoughtless of me to inconvenience you after I cleaned, shopped, and baked for two weeks and have been up since 5:00 a.m. cooking."

Sarah (Gwen's daughter): "Uncle Ed, would you just once make an entrance without complaining, or better yet, say something nice to Mom?"

Ed: "Boy, can't anybody in this house take a joke?"

Gwen then stormed into the kitchen and started banging pots even though everything was already prepared and no pots were needed. Finally, after a few awkward quiet moments, Gwen remembered what she really wanted was not to make her brother wrong but to have a pleasant day, and the only way she was going to get that was if she changed *her* script.

In a few minutes, Gwen calmly emerged from the kitchen and said, "You know, Ed, this is not worth getting upset over." She then paused and looked at Ed again and said, "So how about helping me get everything on the table." To everyone's shock, Ed got up and started putting the food on the table, something he had never done before. Gwen said to be honest, she had never asked him before.

Gwen recounted that the rest of the meal went relatively smoothly, and after dinner, Ed even complimented her on how delicious everything tasted.

Later that evening after the in-town guests went home, Gwen's son Jon asked her why the change of heart? She said, "I just decided that I was no longer going to let Uncle Ed ruin my holidays, and since I could not change him, what I could change was not letting him push my buttons and get upset. Last evening, I thought about what was likely to happen today and planned what I would say and do instead. It just took me a few minutes to turn off my automatic response."

Gwen got clarity about what she really wanted for her holiday before that day. She wanted a pleasant day with her family, and she realized that her past behavior made her an unconscious co-conspirator in the annual *Horrible Holiday* tragedy that usually unfolded. Instead of sticking to her initial goal of having a pleasant day, she reflexively let the goal be changed when her brother walked in.

Not surprisingly, Gwen and Ed had a very long history of this kind of behavior. Did Gwen or Ed consciously produce their *Horrible Holiday* show? No! Their lifelong habits just nudged them to pick up their roles. Roles they had been programmed to play over years of practice.

We are often innocent and unconscious co-conspirators in the plays and stories of our life that do not serve our true intentions or needs. I say "innocent" because it is important that when we discover these unhelpful patterns, we do not beat ourselves up or make others wrong. The patterns in our lives often evolve from past incidents, dynamics, or from perceived threats. The important thing is to recognize them and choose, as Gwen did, to act differently. The goal is to remember that you need to change your own story and script in order to create something different for yourself and others.

Moving Forward to Positive Intent

1. Practice wondering!

When you find yourself assuming the worst about someone's intent, as Gwen did about her brother's actions, stop and ask yourself the "I wonder why" questions.

a. Start with yourself. Here are a few to get you started.
   I wonder why I am feeling this way?
   I wonder why I am not pushing back on this issue and sharing my data?
   I wonder why I am raising my voice?

b. Assess others' words and actions with wonder.
   I wonder why she is ignoring the agenda?
   I wonder why they are repeating this point for a third time?
   I wonder why she is always ten minutes late to this meeting?

Note below what results you achieved from asking the "I wonder why" questions and what insights you gained. The goal here is not to always answer the "I wonder why" question; it is to get in the habit of using the question as a tool to slow down your thinking and choose another path.

2. Different day, different script

What scripts do you want to change in your life? Think about the times when you may be an innocent, unconscious co-conspirator in situations where you desire a different result.

Note a situation below and see if you can't re-create the current script and do something different. Write down where you could say or do something different and what you are willing to try. Remember that the goal here is to disrupt the current pattern, not to do things perfectly right. It might take a few attempts to get the result you want.

Example:

Situation: Monthly Board Meeting

Who is Speaking or Acting	What They and I Said or Did
Boss	"We now need to review and vote on the budget."
Me	"Before we go there, I'd like to discuss the hiring plan."
Boss	"I don't want to discuss the hiring plan until next month." Gave me a stern look.
Me	Got intimidated by how he looked at me and shut down.

What I wish I'd said or done instead

Who is Speaking or Acting	What I Wish I'd Said or Done
Me	Before the meeting—Get supporters for the hiring plan to help me feel more confident and supported. During the meeting—Don't assume that his look means he's angry and continue. Say: "If we wait till next month, it will be too late to fund our critical needs this year."

Who is Speaking or Acting	What I Wish I'd Said or Done

My Situation: _____

Who is Speaking or Acting	What They Said or Did

What I wish I'd said or done instead

Who is Speaking or Acting	What I Wish I'd Said or Done Instead

Stage 2: Traps

STAGE 3

Values and Vision

"If you want to move people, it has to be toward a vision that's positive for them, that taps important values, that gets them something they desire and it has to be presented in a compelling way so that they feel inspired to follow."

Martin Luther King Jr.

Stage 3: Values and Vision

CHAPTER 6

Defining Your Values

Deciding what you really want in life is not easy unless you are someone who has been laser focused since childhood. For many of us, it has been more of a journey of trial and error.

My own path took a number of major turns, from oceanography to business management to logistics, and finally to leadership and executive development. This path was not uncommon to individuals of my generation. No one would have ever charted such a seemingly disjointed path as mine unless they knew my criteria for a job was broader experience, creative flexibility, and autonomy. My vision was to help others clear the *clutter* and enable them to do their best. With that goal, almost any challenging position would have worked for me given the right boss and right conditions, as I mentioned before.

Critical to mustering up the courage to make a request of others is knowing why it is important to you. How will the fulfillment of this request bring you closer to your goal? There are many exercises or activities that can help you more clearly define what you want. Techniques such as writing a manifesto, creating a vision board, trying things out through volunteering, and taking classes are just a few. The important thing is to do something that will help create clarity and open your world to new possibilities that will help you move further along your path.

A value is an important and lasting belief or ideal. It is a principle or standard of behavior you hold in high regard that determines your priorities, motivations, and actions. For example, things like justice, equality, loyalty. Beliefs, on the other hand, are assumptions we hold true that may inform our values. Beliefs, such as that God created the world and stealing is bad, are usually based in religion, and may or may not be based in facts. While both beliefs and values govern our behavior and attitude, values are not based on past information. They are universal, transcend context, and have a strong effect on our day-to-day behavior and character.

Determining Our Values

For the past twenty-five years I have used a process with thousands of leaders to help them identify their values. While some recommend starting with creating a vision, I have found that the best place to start is in defining your core values. Values form the bedrock for our vision to stand on.

Knowing your values creates an internal compass to help you navigate your way through choices, social pressures, and any situation or challenge you encounter. Once you understand what your values are, they generally do not change during your life and they provide a canon or personal yardstick that guides your day-to-day decisions and behavior, allowing you to lead with consistency and integrity.

I had a friend named Rob who worked with me as an oceanographer. Our work involved developing survey maps that would be used to improve navigation and could also be used for invasion in case of war. Rob loved the work of being out on the water, working with the enlisted men and officers, and the foreign travel, but felt disheartened that if there ever was a war, his work could lead to the death of others someday. This job supported his core values of adventure, hard work, and supporting others, but he felt that it also violated his number-one core value, that of respecting and valuing human life.

I had a logistics manager who worked for me on my leadership programs. A few months after sitting through my values exercise, she told me that she was leaving her NASA job because she realized that while she loved working for the agency, her heart was really in helping women in underprivileged communities. She obtained a position with the city coaching women to help them move out of poverty. Her number-one value was service, which she could provide in either position, but her second-highest value was giving back, and she felt she should be in a place where there was a greater need for her abilities.

Our core values are complex and aren't always clear to us. This is what sometimes stops us when we ask for support. If two of your most important values are family and advancement, they can be at odds when you consider taking that next promotion. Clearly the value of advancement is served by the promotion, but how will the promotion affect the time you have to spend with your family? The deciding factor might be in one of your other values that is not yet known to you consciously or in the priority of these two strongly held values.

The following five-step process is designed to help you identify your five highest values and then to make tough choices between those five so you know which one is the most important.

Step 1: Positive meaningful moments

Think of instances when you felt most comfortable and effective. When you were able to be at your best. For example, it may have been when you were working with your children to build a new playground for an underserved community. Or, when you were working with a team to develop a new process that cut processing times in half. Think about what you were doing in these meaningful moments that made you feel good. Write them down in the box below. Try to come up with at least five instances.

Positive Instances
1.
2.
3.
4.
5.

Step 2: Negative meaningful moments

Now consider the times when you were angry or frustrated. What was going on during those times? Why were you feeling that way? What value was being dishonored or challenged? Was it when your boss cut short your presentation and changed the direction of your project before you got to present your findings? Was it when you felt your partner was spending too much on holiday presents after you both worked out a budget and agreed to stick to it? Write these negative meaningful moments below. Again, try to come up with at least five instances.

Negative Instances
1.
2.
3.
4.
5.

Step 3: Identifying common values

What do these different events have in common? Think about the words that represent these positive and negative situations. For example, in positive situations of both building the playground and defining a new process, was it because you were *making a contribution* or because *there was respect among the team members* or because you were *learning something new*? There can be many different reasons for your enjoying the experience, and it will probably be different for each person who also enjoyed that same experience. In the negative situations, were you angry or frustrated because the other person showed a lack of respect *by not fulfilling an agreement,* or was it your *need for certainty* that was upset? Could it also have been that in these cases you felt *trust was broken*?

Think about how these positive and negative instances relate to each other. As you can see from the following example, core values can show up in both positive and negative situations. The values of health and self-respect are honored in the positive situation and violated in the negative situation.

Example

1. Positive Situation	2. Value Honored	3. Negative Situation	4. Value Violated
Getting a promotion	Security	Not fulfilling an agreement	Self-Respect
Hiking on vacation	Health	Being micromanaged	Autonomy
Colleagues appreciating each other's contribution	Self-Respect	Being assigned to a failing project	Accomplish-ment
Donating to the poor	Altruism	Getting the flu	Health

My values

In space #1 below, copy down the instance from your work above that represents the positive situations to you. In space #3 below, copy the instance from your work above that represents the negative situations to you. Now in space #2 note the value that was honored in this situation, and in space #4 note the value that was dishonored.

If you are having trouble identifying the value, see page 94 for a list of values that may help you. Sometimes people have difficulty defining the value that the situation most closely represents. Following is a list of over 100 more common values to help you. Some of these are similar but not exactly the same. Use the word for the value with which you most resonate. There are about 400 values to choose from, so if these 100 do not resonate with you, do an Internet search on **list of core values** for more options.

1. Positive Situation	2. Value Honored	3. Negative Situation	4. Value Violated

Situations you perceive as positive and negative are just one way of defining your core values. Another approach to sorting your values is to be forced to decide between them, which we will do as our final step.

☐ Accomplishment	☐ Courage	☐ Happiness
☐ Achievement	☐ Creativity	☐ Hard Work
☐ Advancement	☐ Dedication	☐ Harmony
☐ Adventure	☐ Dependability	☐ Health
☐ Affection	☐ Determination	☐ Helpfulness
☐ Altruism	☐ Dignity	☐ Honesty
☐ Ambition	☐ Economic	☐ Honor
☐ Authenticity	Security	☐ Humor
☐ Autonomy	☐ Empathy	☐ Hope
☐ Balance	☐ Empowerment	☐ Humility
☐ Beauty	☐ Endurance	☐ Independence
☐ Bravery	☐ Equality	☐ Influence
☐ Brilliance	☐ Excellence	☐ Inner Harmony
☐ Certainty	☐ Exploration	☐ Integrity
☐ Challenge	☐ Fairness	☐ Involvement
☐ Charity	☐ Faith	☐ Joy
☐ Commitment	☐ Fame	☐ Justice
☐ Common Sense	☐ Family	☐ Kindness
☐ Community	☐ Famous	☐ Knowledge
☐ Compassion	☐ Fortitude	☐ Leadership
☐ Competence	☐ Freedom	☐ Learning
☐ Competitiveness	☐ Friendship	☐ Liberty
☐ Confidence	☐ Fun	☐ Love
☐ Connection	☐ Generosity	☐ Loyalty
☐ Contentment	☐ Grace	☐ Mastery
☐ Contribution	☐ Gratitude	☐ Meaningful Work
☐ Cooperation	☐ Growth	☐ Moderation

- ❏ Openness
- ❏ Optimism
- ❏ Order
- ❏ Passion
- ❏ Peace
- ❏ Persistence
- ❏ Personal Development
- ❏ Pleasure
- ❏ Popularity
- ❏ Power
- ❏ Productivity
- ❏ Professionalism
- ❏ Prosperity
- ❏ Purpose
- ❏ Quality
- ❏ Recognition
- ❏ Reputation
- ❏ Respect
- ❏ Responsibility
- ❏ Results-oriented
- ❏ Risk
- ❏ Security
- ❏ Self-Reliance
- ❏ Self-Respect
- ❏ Service
- ❏ Sharing
- ❏ Silence
- ❏ Simplicity
- ❏ Sincerity
- ❏ Spirituality
- ❏ Stability
- ❏ Status
- ❏ Strength
- ❏ Success
- ❏ Sustainability
- ❏ Teamwork
- ❏ Timeliness
- ❏ Tolerance
- ❏ Tranquility
- ❏ Transparency
- ❏ Trust
- ❏ Trustworthy
- ❏ Truth
- ❏ Unity
- ❏ Wealth
- ❏ Wisdom

Step 4: Defining your five nonnegotiables

You probably have a list of ten or more values that are important to you. You now need to sort through these values you defined in Step 3 and identify the five values that are your "nonnegotiables." Nonnegotiables are the values that are not open to compromise. They define who you are and what you stand for in life. Write each of these five values on separate pieces of paper as shown below.

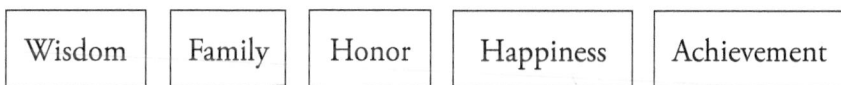

| Wisdom | Family | Honor | Happiness | Achievement |

Before moving on to the last step, take one more minute to look over your values. Are they truly yours? As I mentioned before, there are often other voices in our head from family, friends, and society at large telling us what we *should* want as our values. Is honor really one of your five or did you have a parent or grandparent who was a US Marine and you heard the message of honor in all they did and said, so it feels a part of you now? Maybe for you it is not honor but trustworthiness that resonates more in your heart. If there are values you need to validate, take a few minutes to look up the definitions of these words against other values that may be equally true and pick the one that most closely represents how you feel.

Pause
It is OK to take a break here and spend some time thinking about your values. Go through a few days and see what drives you to take the actions and make the choices you do. It is also perfectly fine to create a first draft of it now and then do some observation and reflection later to decide if you want to make any changes.

Step 5: Prioritizing your top five values

Now, take your five pieces of paper that have your top five values and read the story below. Imagine you are engaging in the following journey with your family or someone you care deeply about. As you reach each decision point, you will need to give up one of your values.

You have won a trip of a lifetime. You can choose to go anywhere in the world. A few hours after your plane departs the borders of civilization, you hit a storm and the plane needs to make an emergency landing in a remote area where there is a tiny airport. The pilot announces that the plane is inoperable, and in order to depart it and find alternate transportation, the local government requires payment of one value. Pick the value you are going to give up and put it face down.

You have departed the plane and paid your landing fee, but you now are told that there is a deadly virus in the area, and in order to travel safely through the country and proceed on your journey, you will have to purchase a health kit that will keep you all safe. The cost of this health kit for your party is one value. Please choose your next value you will give up and put it face down on top of the one you already gave up.

You now need to arrange for passage across a treacherous mountain range to the larger city where you can get transportation either to your vacation destination or back home. The local government has arranged for buses to transport you by the only route that is possible, but you will need to pay. The cost again is one value. Please put this value face down on your pile.

You now proceed on the road. After an hour, a group of locals blocks the road. You learn these locals are a notorious group of criminals that often attack buses and have been known to kill people if their demands aren't met. The cost of safe passage for you and your party is one value. Please put this value face down on the pile.

You now have one value left. Hold on to this value tightly and it will see you safely home or to your vacation destination.

This story involves a forced decision process to find the priority of your five core values. This priority becomes important when you need to choose between two tightly held values that may in any moment appear to be in conflict. For example, if you have the values of certainty and advancement, which way will you lean when you are offered a new job that provides the opportunity to do a number of things you have never tried before? If advancement is a higher priority than certainty, you will probably accept the job and then work on gaining the information you need to be successful very quickly. If certainty is a higher priority than advancement, you may forgo this opportunity and work on building the new skills you will need before moving up.

The wonderful part of asking for what you need is that even if certainty is your highest priority, you may not have to wait. You may find you can say "yes" to this advancement opportunity *and* ask the hiring official for the support you need to quickly gain the knowledge and skills needed for this new challenge. This support may be in the form of a mentor, a coach, a training program, or just access to information. If the support is not possible, then waiting may be the best option for you.

Moving Forward to Defining Your Values

Congratulations, you have completed your values work!

CHAPTER 7

Creating Your Vision

Once you have identified and prioritized your values, the next step is to clarify your personal vision. A vision statement creates a picture of the future that helps motivate us to move forward. If done well, a vision statement will paint a vivid picture in your mind of what success looks like. This is the big picture of your life. It defines who you want to be and what you want to accomplish. Some of the most well-known vision statements are those of corporations or their CEOs.

The vision is your "why." It gives meaning to your life and inspires and shapes your understanding of what you want to do over time. Creating a vision may take time to refine. In coaching leaders, I found that most people start with a vision statement that feels right in the moment, but then it unfolds the more they think about it. It tends to be like the classic description of the onion. As you think about your vision, you will continue to uncover deeper layers of understanding what is important to you. Each layer takes you closer to your true self and what you really want to achieve in life.

"Build the best product, cause no unnecessary harm, use business to inspire and implement solutions to the environmental crisis."
—Patagonia

"To be the best quick service restaurant experience. Being the best means providing outstanding quality, service, cleanliness, and value, so that we make every customer in every restaurant smile."
—McDonald's

"To serve as a leader, live a balanced life, and apply ethical principles to make a significant difference."
—Denise Morrison, CEO, Campbell Soup Company

The following questions will help you begin this process of defining your vision. I strongly encourage you to find quiet space to think about your answers to these questions. As mentioned previously, there are many voices that tell you what you *should* want, so be sure you answer these questions for you rather than what anyone else wants for you. As you answer these questions, think about how the answers make you feel. More on that later after you create your initial vision statement. If it has been a few days since you have completed your values exercise, go back and reacquaint yourself with these values and how they make you feel. It is critical that you feel alignment between your values and vision. Your values should strongly influence your responses to these questions.

Step 1: Identify what you enjoy

1. Name five things that you enjoy that if you had to give them up would make you feel sad or incomplete.

   1.
   2.
   3.
   4.
   5.

2. What three to five things do you do every day that give you joy and make you feel complete?

   1.

   2.

   3.

   4.

   5.

3. If you did not have to work, what would you love to do with your life?

4. What talents and abilities do you have that you love using?

5. Who do you enjoy being around? What kind of people? What do they do for you?

Step 2: Identify what matters in life

1. What life do you want to have lived?

2. If you could accomplish great things, given resources, support, and the best circumstances, what would they be?

3. What do you want to change about the world? What contribution do you want to make?

4. What do you want to be remembered for?

5. What would you regret not having done?

Step 3: Identify categories and themes

As you did with your values, look for categories and themes that are emerging from your answers above. Make a list of the themes that matter to you. For example, it might be helping others, being sought after for your expertise, making a contribution, spending time with family, using your talents, etc.

Go back and review your values. Notice how the themes above reflect your core values? If your core values are not reflected in these themes, note what is missing? Don't overthink this; just add the missing pieces. As your vision emerges, this will become clearer.

Step 4: Write your vision statement

Think of this step as a no-holds-barred exercise. Let yourself have everything you want in life. Most importantly, it must motivate and inspire you. Start with individual sentences that embrace your desires and your values. As you write these sentences, what do you feel? Do you get a twinge of excitement or maybe fear? Do you get a little misty, thinking about what you are putting down on paper? If you do, you are on the right track. This means that you are hitting the core of what is important to you. If not, keep refining each sentence until it really "gets to you."

After going through this process with thousands of leaders for several decades I found that unless they had done this work before, what these professionals wrote initially was closer to what society or their parents wanted for them, and that's OK. Again, this is a journey. Most of the leadership programs I ran were nine to twelve months, and for almost all the participants, their vision statement at the end of the program was very different from where they started, so again you are in good company.

The following describes three ways that will help you to move your vision forward:

Make it *provoking*

A vision statement should be exciting and convey emotion and passion. It should provoke, energize, motivate, and compel you to take action. The origin of the word emotion is "to move" from the old French; it means to "stir up." Your vision statement should stir you to think and act differently to get what you really want out of life.

Make it in the *present*

One more key requirement is for you to write your vision statement in the present tense as if it is already happening, as though you are already living it. When we write vision statements in the future tense, we tend to delay getting started because it is not real to us yet. Writing in the present tense, we trick our subconscious mind into believing it is already happening. This is no longer something we are wishing for in the future, it is happening right now!

Make it *positive*

Write your vision statement using only positive words. Positive words generate energy. They help us focus on creating a "toward" state versus avoiding something negative. If you say, "We never disappoint our customers," it has a very different message and motivation than "We always delight our customers." Or, "I am not afraid of new experiences," versus "I embrace new experiences." You will go where your mind goes, so give it the words it needs to move you forward and stay motivated.

The Three Powerful Ps in a Vision Statement:

Provoking
Present
Positive

Below are a few examples of vision statements that might help you get started. As you read these, note what values you are hearing. Can you tell what is important to these individuals?

"As a positive influence, I create programs for seniors that enable them to share their wisdom and talents with children. I never give up on my goals and encourage others who may feel like giving up. I enjoy great health and vitality."

"I am a motivational leader who develops inspiring programs that enable others to make their greatest contribution. I show gratitude to God every day and I am someone my children look up to with pride."

"I work internationally helping women in developing countries create small businesses that support their families and community. I have reached the peak of my career and am a successful consultant to many who are looking to fund small businesses."

One technique that tends to help individuals maintain clear thinking is writing sentences that only include one key thought. Let's take the last example above. In this example, the three key parts of this vision statement are:

- Working internationally to support women's small businesses,
- At the peak of my career, and
- Successfully consulting to fund small businesses.

These three thoughts are easy to understand and recall as opposed to long, compound sentences that confuse the mind and are harder to remember. After working with David Rock for several years, I have become convinced that his guidance of "no more than three" items or thoughts is best. Think about it. If your vision statement is difficult for you to recall, what are the chances it will motivate and inspire you or anyone else? If you have trouble remembering it, you may associate your vision with a painful experience and thus avoid thinking or acting on it. Not only do clear, concise concepts make it easy for you to remember and embrace, they can also be quickly and easily communicated to others from whom you are seeking support.

Now it is time for you to write your own vision statement. Again, if this is your first try, don't worry about getting it perfect; just write what comes to mind. Stream of consciousness is a great way to start.

My Vision Statement

Step 5: Reflect and clarify
===========================

Reflect on the vision you wrote. Again, think about whose voice you hear when you read it. Is it your parents, your boss, your preacher, society? Is it truly yours or is it something that you been told you "*should*" want? Many of our core wants and values come from how we were raised and what we connect to, so having an assertion in your vision statement that may be the same as your parents is fine, as long as it is *also* truly *yours*.

Pause
I revisit this caution of ensuring this is your own voice often because my experience has taught me that isolating your own voice from those of others and society can be very hard. It can take a lot of conscious thinking to hear your own voice when there are so many messages vying for your attention.

How does your vision statement make you feel when you read it? Some people end up with more of a laundry list and several paragraphs in their first attempt to write a vision statement. Many are worried that they will leave something important out, and that's great for a first step. However, we know we cannot hold more than three to four things in our brain at any given time, so refining this statement down to its core essence over time will make it easy to recall and much more powerful. It will also make it more likely to become part of your daily life. Short and clear AND rich and powerful vision statements are easy to remember and communicate.[31] Disney's vision is simply "*To make people happy.*" I imagine every one of Disney's over 200,000 employees can not only recall the company vision, but they also think about how they can achieve it every day.

Step 6: Speak your vision

Once you have a vision statement that feels right to you, find several people to speak it to. In my programs I have my participants initially speak their vision statement to at least five other people. Speaking a commitment out loud does several things. First, it makes it real. This is not a theoretical exercise. This is your vision for your life, and you might as well get started right now on moving in that direction. What you speak has power. Second, speaking your vision helps you get closer to knowing if this is really core for you. The more you say it, the more clarity you get. And third, when you share your hopes and dreams with others, you vastly expand the possibility of getting their support even before you have made a request.

> *"Words are our most inexhaustible source of magic."*
> *J. K. Rowling*

My experience with people I coach is that when they get to a point where the vision truly reflects who they are, it actually becomes a bit hard to say it out loud. They tend to pause or get a catch in their throat. There is actually a physical response that they cannot hide from themselves. If they are able to speak it out loud and it easily rolls off their tongue like they are reading a script, it is often what they think they are supposed to say. At this point I will usually say something provocative like "No, that's not it." They often get angry at my response and start to argue with me and explain why it is their vision. Usually in the explanation, they begin to talk themselves out of it or realize there is something even more core that they are not yet saying.

Put some thought into the people to whom you will want to speak your vision. I prefer for the people I coach to speak their vision to individuals they do not know very well, maybe a colleague or casual friend. When doing this exercise, I recommend that you choose people who do not have a vested interest in your vision yet. You will probably need the support of your colleagues, friends, and family to realize your vision, but not at this stage. At this point this exercise is just for you. You just want to hear yourself say it out loud to a real audience to see how *you* feel when you say it. Is it really you? Do you own it? Are you motivated to start acting on it?

This may sound a bit scary, but I encourage my students to use their vision as their introduction. Think of the number of times you meet new people and have to introduce yourself. You are likely to have hundreds of opportunities within a year to garner support for your vision, but only if you share it.

For example, "Hi, my name is Jarrod Patel, and I am an accountant with XYZ. My real passion, though, is to use my experience to mentor high school students to develop good lifelong financial habits." You may or may not be actually mentoring at this point, but that's OK. This could be an opportunity to make a request. "I'd love to hear any ideas you have on how I might move forward with this idea." Asking is where we are going next.

Moving Forward to Create Your Vision

Congratulations again! You have completed your vision work.

STAGE 4

If You Don't Ask, the Answer Is No

"Never apologize for asking for what you
need; if you don't ask—the answer will
always be no."

Rachel Wolchin

Stage 4: If You Don't Ask, the Answer Is Always No

CHAPTER 8

Why Do People Say Yes?

As I mentioned in the preface, experts now say that the most important capability of a leader is self-awareness. "Self-awareness at work often gets overlooked because we see the consequences of self-awareness—or a lack thereof—and don't often identify self-awareness leadership as the root cause of those consequences. For example, we all want leaders who are good listeners, who are able to see both sides of an argument, and who know when to delegate and when to take a more hands-on approach. The skill behind each of those capabilities is self-awareness."[32] That was why the first three stages of this book were all about helping you gain a better understanding of yourself.

The work you have done to reach this point is designed to go deeper than just recognizing your strengths and weaknesses. It has been about uncovering a narrative that, regardless of knowing your strengths and weaknesses, has the power to affect your thoughts and actions. It's been about having tools to release those traps, and without those old stories getting in the way, helping you identify your core values and shape a clear vision so you can get what you really want. In this part, we will look at how we can best help others say yes to our requests.

If you are the type of leader who has resisted asking others for help, you might be prone to thinking that a request has to be for something very important or highly significant. When asking for help or favors, it is useful to start small for two reasons. First, making a number of small requests helps to build your asking muscle. It helps you get comfortable with asking on issues that will not have a major impact on your life. When your neighbor says no to your request to borrow his lawn mower while yours is in the shop, it is inconvenient and probably irritating, but not career threatening.

The second reason to start small has to do with building a connection to the other person so that they want to say yes. To better understand why asking for something first versus giving something works, we need to look at a cognitive bias commonly called the Benjamin Franklin effect.[33]

The Benjamin Franklin effect

In his biography, Franklin describes how during the creation of the Constitution he was able to get a rival legislator on his side. Rather than trying to persuade, flatter, or bribe him, Franklin asked to borrow a rare book which he knew the legislator was in possession of. The rival agreed, and shortly afterward Franklin returned the book with a note telling him how much he enjoyed it. When the two met next, Franklin's rival was more civil and showed more willingness to work with him.

> This psychological effect has to do with something we discussed earlier, cognitive dissonance. Our brain craves consistency, so we will change our attitudes and behaviors to resolve tensions, or dissonance between our beliefs and our actions.

Since the rival legislator knew he only lent books to people he liked, his brain began to see Franklin as an ally and began to focus on things that supported that belief rather than their differences.

While this may at first sound counterintuitive, asking someone to do a favor for you can have a powerful effect. Logically it seems to make sense that by asking someone to do something for us, we might actually cause him or her to dislike us. In fact, research shows that a person who has already performed a favor for us is more likely to do another favor for us. People are willing to be persuaded when the action is consistent with something they have done before.

Just as we create our own stories for why we don't ask for what we need and want in life, we also create stories and rationale for saying yes or no to a request. I am not saying that you should go around just thinking of what people can do for you, but you should not be afraid to ask first, because it has the power to build a connection and create an ally.

A key element of the successful leadership programs I design includes the requirement for participants to articulate what we call their Leadership Story as a way to build connections and motivate others to support their goals. To do this, participants first need to get clear about their vision and values, so if you have done the work in the preceding chapters, you are ready for this.

Leadership in this context refers to a passion and commitment for the thing you are trying to achieve. I personally like the Wikipedia definition of leadership as "a process of social influence in which a person can enlist the aid and support of others in the accomplishment of a common and ethical task."[34] In making requests of others, that is exactly what we are doing: enlisting their aid and support toward realizing a common goal.

A powerful request has four elements designed to spur others to connect to your vision and take action: alignment, results, action, and brevity. All of these elements are there to make it as easy as possible for the person you are asking to say yes!

CHAPTER 9

Making Powerful Requests

Step 1: Create alignment

We all have experiences that have shaped our leadership, that helped define our core values. These are what drive your desire to achieve your vision and the reason why you became a leader and are putting yourself out there and asking for help. Alignment is about finding the intersection between what you seek for yourself or your organization and what others seek.

Many of the technical leaders I knew at NASA loved what they were doing as employees working on projects. They struggled with giving up the hands-on work they enjoyed and were good at to move into leadership roles. The ones who made the most successful transitions were those who made the moves because they knew the position they were moving to would allow them to influence and achieve their vision. There was something greater driving their decision than money, status, or the minor perks that came with public service leadership. They also knew what they were giving up and made a conscious decision to leave that technical, hands-on work behind rather than trying to do it all.

One story that always stands out for me is that of a safety engineer at NASA. He was your typical logical, data-driven, wicked smart engineer who did not have time for the *touchy-feely* stuff. He struggled greatly with finding alignment with his team. He would give them data, statistics, and failure rates, and thought that once his team saw the data, they would understand why he was trying to make these critical changes and embrace them. This leader was previously an expert at generating this type of data, and so in trying to influence his team, it was no wonder he relied on what he knew best. Unfortunately, what he needed as a leader to get his team on board was a different set of skills. Ones he was not yet comfortable using.

On the final night of our weeklong workshop I asked him to have dinner so we could talk more about why he was struggling with his Leadership Story. At one point while we talked, he said, "You know, I just don't know why I can't get my team behind me on this." I asked him again to think about the core values he identified for himself this week and see if he could find a connection between them and what he was trying to accomplish. He paused for a long moment and then said, "You know, every day as I enter the building, I walk down the hallway that has the pictures of the astronauts who are currently in orbit. As I walk down that hall, I touch their frames to remind myself that their lives are in my hands and I have to do all I can every day to ensure they come home safely to their families." In this moment we both had tears in our eyes. You can't be too surprised to learn that family, safety, and community were his top three values. I asked him if he thought his team shared his values and if they would relate to his story of protecting the astronauts so they come safely home to their families. He said he was sure they did. He started his next meeting by telling his team the story he told me and soon got the support he needed.

Helping others see how we care about the same things, have similar experiences, and share a common background or desire to right the same wrong works to create a connection that says we are on the same team. Once we feel we are part of a group, our identity and theirs becomes aligned, and we have a natural desire to enhance and protect that identity because it is also our own.

Affinity or in-group bias, which we discussed earlier, is our human tendency to perceive people who are similar to us more positively than those different from us. This feeling of familiarity or sameness has been shown to result in greater trust, more willingness to cooperate, greater empathy, and a preferential allocation of resources (or help). Our preference for people "like us" has important ramifications in our ability to get a positive response when asking others for their support.

"When people have a common goal, their brains process things differently."[35]
David Rock and Khalil Smith

That's what alignment in this powerful request model means—connecting in a way that touches and moves us—and it requires us to be a bit vulnerable. Going to the root of what matters to us, as I mentioned before, can cause a visceral response, and that can scare us because we may not be comfortable expressing our emotions or ready to put ourselves out there. But it is worth it. Emotion can be the fuel that helps others to move in the direction of supporting you and your ability to accomplish your vision and your organization's goals.

When someone tells you not just what is important to them but why it is important and relates it to their values and experience, you cannot help but feel connected. As a leader, your power in this moment is being your authentic self—revealing what is really important to you and why it may also be important to them.

There is a very good chance you either know or have a sense that the person you are making a request of already has a connection between your values or vision, because you have chosen to ask them. You would not have chosen this person out of thin air. Even if you don't know them, trust your instincts. Remember, even if they say no, you will be no further behind than you were before.

Rewrite your core values and vision below:

My top five core values:

My vision:

Now with these in mind, answer the questions below:

Who is the person or persons I want to ask for help?	

What do I want from this person?	

To uncover alignment, think: Why them?

There must be some particular reason why you are asking a person for their support. What makes you think they can help? Do they have the skill, knowledge, or experience you need? Have their actions or accomplishments personally inspired or impacted you? We all love to be validated for our hard work; however, in this case it is to help set the context for the other person, not just to compliment them. It is letting them know why you are asking them, specifically! If you are not quite sure of the connection, don't make something up. It's OK to admit you are not quite clear on the connection or even what to ask and just frame your vision and see how they respond.

Why this person?	

According to Heidi Grant, "what people really want to give is unique or, to use the technical term, 'nonsubstitutable' help. Help that only they can give. Because the more unique the help, the more closely tied it is to who they are."[36] Giving that which only we can give connects the act of giving to our concept of ourselves. It gives us a glimpse into how distinctive and special we are. Help people see how their willingness to help you makes them special and how their efforts will make a unique contribution to what you both want to accomplish.

Step 2: Defining results

Research shows that having a connection to something bigger than ourselves makes us happier and healthier.[37] We are wired for much more than just our own survival. We want to know that what we do, the effort we make and the actions we take, will make an impact and produce the results we envisioned. Those results give meaning to our life.

Results in this model need to be observable, measurable, and valuable. They benefit not just you, but they also connect to the greater good or bigger picture.

I served on a women's scholarship selection committee, and based on the candidates' essays I classified the applications into two categories: those that inspired me and made me want to support them and those that did not. The difference was in the impact they described as to what they wanted to do with their college degrees.

For some applicants, the scholarship was a way to get their degree which would lead to a great job in a field they loved and thus help increase the number of women in that field. The inspiring ones wanted to get their degree to change the world. They had big plans that would not end with just getting a job and being counted, but included goals such as decreasing infant mortality in third world countries or finding ways to provide micro-financing to small businesses that would otherwise not qualify. To be very honest, I felt much better selecting an applicant who wanted to change the world, knowing that the time

I spent reviewing these scholarship applications might have even an infinitesimal part in decreasing infant mortality or providing needed micro-financing.

Now every request you make may not be at the level of changing the world, but I bet almost every request has a connection to something larger than yourself. Those applicants who wanted to get a good job and be counted probably also had bigger ideas but did not have the experience or awareness to think about, or express, their goals that way.

I have found that making this connection to a greater purpose, something that gives our lives more meaning, can be very challenging for people, even for parents, teachers, medical professionals, those working in public service, etc., where everything they do in their jobs tends to be for the benefit of others and creating a better tomorrow. It often feels far too big to describe or they are still carrying one of the inhibiting stories that limits how they see themselves being able to have an impact.

This is why I love the "Five Whys" technique originally developed by Sakichi Toyoda, as it forces us to think about the connections between even the smallest action and the greater impact. This technique is mostly used for analyzing the root cause of problems, but I have found that it is also highly useful in helping us see and frame for others the impact they can have on your efforts.

Even with something as simple as asking your assistant to edit a document, you can think about the bigger impact and let them know how important the work is and that their efforts matter. Let's look at an example.

1. Why edit the document?

   If this document is well edited, it will quickly go through the review process.

2. Why is it important to quickly go through the review process?
   Because the information needs to get to pharmacists before the new generation of this drug is released.

3. Why is it important to get it to pharmacists before the new generation of this drug is released?
   Because our updated research shows that the first generation of this medicine may not work for certain patients.

4. Why is it important that the drug protocols used are effective for all patients?
   Because if the medication is not effective, there are others these patients could take that would work better.

5. What does it matter if it is not as effective as other drugs?
   If patients are not taking the most effective drug, it could lead to heart attacks and death.

Now, you probably would not go through the Five Whys with your assistant, but when you are asking them to edit the document, you might mention that this information is critical for pharmacists to ensure they are recommending medications that will prevent heart attacks and possibly save lives. How much more engaged might your assistant be if they know that what they do today could save a life tomorrow?

You don't always have to go through the Five Whys to uncover the greater purpose behind your request; you may already know it but are just not in the habit of articulating it. Most leaders have a better view of the bigger picture, so let your employees in on it. Even if you intuitively know the ultimate result, if the request is important, the Five Whys can help ensure that your reasoning holds together. When you go through this process, you can find the flaws in your thinking, if there are any.

Results need to paint a vivid picture of the future you want to create and to let others know how they can be a part of it. If a result is compelling, others will be more willing to say yes and work with you to be a part of that vision.

Build your Five Why story below. Identify a situation you are dealing with or a challenge you are facing. I have found that this is a great exercise to do with your team because others might have different insights and observations that help explain what is going on.

Why?	
Why?	
Why?	
Why?	
Why?	

You will find times where even though you have provided a crystal clear story and have shown the alignment, your employees may not get inspired. In this case I recommend learning more about what inspires and motivates them. Remember, every brain has different wiring, and you may have to search for another path.

Step 3: Move to action

The person you are asking wants to know what you are planning to do, the action you plan to take, and how they can be a part of it. Specifically, what you need from them to achieve the desired result.

The strategy here is to make your request quick and easy to do. If you want them to make a call to refer you to someone, look up the number ahead of time and offer to provide it so they don't have to look it up. If you want them to write a letter of reference, let them know exactly which areas they should address and give them a few prompts of why you think they are the best person to provide this information.

A colleague of mine whom I worked with six years prior asked for a letter of recommendation focusing on her ability to reduce costs and improve efficiency. I asked her to send me her résumé and tell me why she was asking me, and I was glad I did. I had completely forgotten I nominated her for an award that she won for her creativity in reducing processing times from two weeks to several hours. In reviewing her résumé, I remembered a number of other projects we did together that I could mention in the letter.

Think about those emails you get where you just have to click a button or copy someone. Do you do it right away just to get it out of your in-box? Now think of an email you get asking for a report you did a while ago, and you don't actually remember what you called it or where it would be on your computer. If your boss is not breathing down your neck for it, what are the chances you will stop what you are doing and get to it right away?

We humans tend toward what is called availability bias, which means we make decisions based on information that is most readily available to us. If your request is something that is easy and the person has what they need to accomplish your request, it is easier to just do it than to put it off or say no.

Accomplishing something quickly activates our reward response and gives us a quick hit of dopamine that makes us feel good. On the other hand, saying no often makes us feel bad. We tend to feel guilty. But it goes even deeper. It can cause us to question whether we are a nice person, even though all evidence to the contrary may say we are. So, when you make it easy for someone to say yes, honoring your request can feel like a gift to them!

If someone says no, you can still give that person the *dopamine gift*. Ask them if they have any ideas on what you might do as a next step, if they can refer you to someone else, or maybe recommend a video, a book, or an article. This way you have helped them easily contribute and you have a way forward.

> "Most people never ask. And that's what separates, sometimes, the people that do things from the people that just dream about them."[38]
> Steve Jobs

The If-Then tool

Since you have gotten this far into the book, you should be becoming well aware of your stories and the traps that are likely to get in your way. We have looked at how using neutral language and assuming positive intent can help. Next we need a tool proven to help you make the changes you desire: the If-Then tool.

If-Then is a tool that has been proven to help individuals overcome old stories and change habits. Psychologist Peter Gollwitzer discovered the power of If-Then in the mid-1990s, and it has been shown to more than double the success rate of individual efforts to implement lasting change. In over a hundred studies on everything from diet and exercise to negotiation and time management, the If-Then tool has shown that deciding in advance when and where you will take specific actions can dramatically increase your success rate.

There are two steps to using If-Then. The first step is to recognize the response you want to change: the IF part of the equation. The second step is to decide what you will do instead: the THEN part of the process.

The If-Then-And-Ask variation

Since our focus is on asking, I have taken this model one more step and added *and-ask*, to remind us to not just make an internal adjustment to our thinking but to remember to use this to build our asking muscle.

SCARF, Our Stories, and If-Then-And-Ask

David Rock's SCARF© model is a way of understanding the five domains of social experience that our brain sees as threat and reward. Each of the eight stories mentioned earlier fits into this model. The five domains include:

Status *Our importance in relation to others*	#1 We are afraid of what others will think.
	#2 We get to be right or make others wrong.

Certainty *Our ability to predict the future*	#3 We don't really know what we want.
	#4 We are afraid that getting what we want may change our lives or our current stability.
	#8 We don't believe our efforts will make a difference.
Autonomy *Our perception of our ability to exert control over our environment*	#5 We fear that if others know what we want, they will do something to sabotage our efforts, talk us out of it, try to control the direction, or tell us what to do.
Relatedness *Our feeling of security in our relationship with others*	#6 We fear rejection. If they say no, we hear it as a rejection of us, not just a rejection of our request.
Fairness *Our sense of transparency and clear expectations*	#7 We are actually seeking reciprocity from someone; looking for a person to acknowledge that they owe us for past favors or efforts.

SCARF gives us a language to understand the often-unconscious perceived threats that may be driving our behavior. These are simply our current default approach to deal with asking for what we need and want. The good news is this awareness can now help us design strategies that allow us to overcome our threat responses and become more adept at asking for what we need. To see how this works, let's put it in context with the SCARF model and the resistance we might face to the eight stories we told at the start of this book.

<u>Status</u>: If the stories that hold us back are:

#1: We are afraid of what others will think, or
#2: We get to be right or make others wrong.

Our story can be one of having courage or acknowledging that no one knows everything. Following are examples of stories people I coach have created when their status feels threatened.

"IF I think others will consider me dumb when I ask a question, THEN I will tell myself that asking for this information will make me smarter so I can continue to stay at the top of my game, AND ASK the question."

"IF I am feeling like the person will not respect me, THEN I will remind myself that most people are honored when you acknowledge their expertise, AND ASK for a recommendation on what I can do as a next step."

<u>Certainty</u>: If the stories that hold us back are:

#3: We don't really know what we want;
#4: We are afraid that getting what we say we want may change our lives or our current stability; or
#8: We don't believe our efforts will make a difference.

We can remind ourselves that if the person says yes, we still have control over how we will proceed and at what pace. If-Then stories I have heard that support certainty include:

"IF fear of change holds me back, THEN I will create a list of the good things that can come out of getting my request met, AND ASK for my partner to hold me accountable for achieving the goal I set."

"IF I am afraid that my friends or family will not support my career move, THEN I will remind myself of all the support they have given me in the past, AND ASK for help in investigating good neighborhoods near my new job."

Autonomy: If our story is:

#5: We fear that if others know what we want, they will do something to sabotage our efforts, talk us out of it, try to control the direction, or tell us what to do.

We can recall all the parts of our life where we currently have control and how this would be one of many areas where we will decide what is best for ourselves. Examples include:

"IF I am afraid that my parents will not support my traveling to India alone, THEN I will choose to first talk to people who I know will be excited for me AND ASK them to come with me when I talk to my parents."

"IF I am afraid my colleagues will sabotage my efforts to get promoted, THEN I will remind myself of all the good I can do for them in a higher position so I think of them as on my side and not the enemy, AND ASK them what it would take for them to support me."

Relatedness: If our story is:

#6: We fear rejection. If they say no, we hear it as a rejection of us, not just a rejection of our request.

We need a story that reminds us that the people who really care about us will continue to be in our lives no matter what dreams we choose to follow.

"IF I fear my best friend will not support my new career, THEN I will remind myself of how long we have been friends and how much she has backed me in the past, AND ASK her to respect and support my decision."

"IF my family asserts a different political perspective than mine, THEN when we have conflicts I will just listen to their concerns and try to understand why they feel that way, AND ASK them to do the same."

Fairness: If our story is:

#7: We are actually seeking reciprocity from someone; looking for a person to acknowledge that they owe us for past favors or efforts.

We may want to remind ourselves that mind reading is a very rare gift and that the person we want to reciprocate may need more information on how they can support us.

"IF I begin to feel taken advantage of by a family member, THEN I will remind myself that they are not able to read my mind, AND ASK them to complete one specific task by the end of the day."

"IF I do not feel that I am being treated equitably when high-visibility assignments are being made, THEN I will remind myself that I need to let my boss know I am interested in this type of assignment, AND ASK for a commitment to receive equal consideration for the next assignment."

Having a replacement story is a great way of reprogramming the thinking that may be holding us back, but we also need to take action to get what we want. Once our thinking stops holding us back, we need to decide on the action we will take or the request we will make to move to the next level.

What old story or stories are still holding you back from asking for help? And what will be your If-Then-and-Ask strategy if these stories arise?

Story holding me back:
If-Then-and-Ask strategy:

Story holding me back:
If-Then-and-Ask strategy:

As you are building your new asking muscles, let others help reinforce your efforts. Identify people in your life, maybe one at home and one at work or somewhere else, and fill them in on your If-Then strategy. Report to them on your progress and ask them to point out opportunities when you forget. Make sure this is someone who has your best interest at heart and cares about you, so you feel safe. And when they do point out your missed opportunities, remember you asked for their help, so your only response is Thank you!

My If-Then-and-Ask coach:

Step 4: Be brief

At this point I want to emphasize the need for brevity or being succinct in your request. As mentioned before, our conscious brain has limited capacity and it takes a lot of mental energy to process new ideas. That's why you need to make your request vivid and at the same time clear and void of extraneous details. You have their attention, now don't lose it by rambling on. The average attention span is now eight seconds,[39] which means you need to get your listener's attention quickly. If they get fully engaged or want more details, they will ask for them. Often, we think that in order for others to take us seriously, we have to give them every detail. Not so. What you need to do is quickly and powerfully get to the point by cutting to the heart of the issue using as few words as possible.

This means not just hoping you will say the right thing, but actually practicing your request. In NASA's leadership programs, we had people practice their stories to get them down to three minutes. These days I would say three minutes is an enormous luxury most people do not have, so I now recommend 30 seconds.

You want to set the context so they can connect it to the reference maps already in the brain. A great way to do this is to think about how your vision connects to theirs.

What is the essence of my request?	
How can I shorten my request?	

Focus on the what, not the how

As you ask for help, keep your eye on the goal, the *what*, but be open to the *how*. As you get people engaged in your vision, you will probably get new ideas that will cause your plans to evolve over time. Think of this evolution not as changing your plan but growing your resources, network, and the possibility of what you can accomplish. If you have strong autonomy needs and your story is #5, that others will try to control your choices, this will be challenging and you will need to have a strong If-Then plan in place.

Speaking of autonomy, remember that just as we are more motivated to act when we have control and can make our own choices, so too are others. If people need to feel that what they do is a unique reflection of who they are, when possible give them choices. As long as they are helping you move your goal forward, be open to how they can support you.

Moving Forward to Planning and Making Powerful Requests

Congratulations! If you've done the work in this chapter, you are ready to make your powerful request. If you struggled with any of the questions in this chapter, take a look at the example below.

Values

My Values				
Teamwork	Growth	Productivity	Caring	Integrity

Vision

My Vision	To improve employee productivity by 90 percent by making software changes intuitively obvious to the user and significantly reducing or eliminating the need for online training.

Alignment

Person I want to ask for help	The head of media planning

What do I want from this person?	I want her to support me when I introduce a new procedure to the CIO that makes software engineers responsible for the full project cycle, including training.
Why this person?	She is someone I have respected for her ability to influence others. She frames issues clearly. She is also a champion of improving company productivity.

Results

My Five Whys:	Problem: Our company loses two thousand hours of productivity whenever we upgrade our systems.
	1. *Why do we lose these hours when we do system upgrades?* Because new and existing software features are not intuitively obvious to users and it takes time for them to figure out the new way of doing things, or they need to take online training to learn the new features, which takes them away from their regular work.
	2. *Why are new and existing software features not intuitively obvious to users?* The software engineers design the systems without sufficient customer input.

My Five Whys:	3. *Why don't the software engineers get more input from their customers?* Because getting customer input slows down the development time, which is the only part of the project cycle for which the engineering department is accountable.
	4. *Why is full implementation not part of the software department's project cycle?* Because previous management made the training department responsible for that part of project deployment.
	5. *Why did previous management make the training department responsible for that part of deployment?* Because the software engineers were not good at communicating with the customers.

Action

What story is still holding me back from asking for help?	I don't believe it will make any difference. I do not have the position or credibility with leadership yet that they will consider I know what I'm talking about.

What is my If-Then-and-Ask strategy if this story arises?	IF this story arises, THEN I will remind myself that one of our key corporate goals this year is to improve productivity, and the head of media planning has this as a critical element on her performance plan AND ASK her for help in strengthening my pitch to address her concerns and make it presentable to the CIO.
Who will be my If-Then-and-Ask coach?	My colleague, Bill, who will be part of my proposal team.

Be Brief

What is the essence of my request?	I request that I be authorized to pilot a new approach to software deployment by making the software engineers responsible for the entire project cycle. I believe by providing enhanced communication skills, the engineers can work more effectively with the customers to define their requirements up front and design systems that are more intuitive. This will reduce the time required for the customers to learn the new system by 90 percent.
How can I shorten my request?	I request approval for a pilot project to change the way we develop and deploy software that can improve productivity by 90 percent. This can be achieved by building engineers' communication skills to ensure products are intuitively easy for customers to use.

As a planning tool and checklist

Clearly there is a lot in this chapter and it breaks the rule of three or four items you can hold in your head at one time, so it is best to use this as a planning tool and a checklist. First, as a planning tool, to ensure you have included everything that is important to make your request as powerful as possible. Second, if you fail to get what you hoped for, check the table below and see what you missed. Without including all the parts of the model, your chances of getting what you really need could be compromised.

If Missing	What You Get
Values	Indifference
Vision	Confusion
Alignment	Detachment
Results	Lack of focus
Action	Inertia
Brevity	Inattention

What if I still get a maybe or a no?

If the dopamine does not kick in right away, don't give up. Some people need time to process their decisions, so give them the space they need. A no or maybe now may lead to a future yes.

If you get a maybe or some other non-specific commitment, be sure before you end the conversation to ask them if it would be OK if you check back; and if they say yes, ask when would be a good time. If they equivocate or say something like "I'll get back to you," assume good intent, check the table above for what you may have missed, *and* if you find nothing missing, move on. They may actually get back to you, which would be great, but there is also a chance they may just be one of those people who can't say the word "no" even when they do not have any intention of following up.

If you get a no, again assume good intent and move on. I encourage you to move on, because you do not want one person to stop your momentum. If there is only one person who can grant your request, such as your boss, then I encourage you to consider two things. First, the timing of your request. Was this really the best time to make this request? What else is going on at this time that could make it hard for him or her to say yes? If it was not a good time, can you think of when you may have a better opportunity in the future? Second, does a no violate one of your core values? This is a much larger concern. If it does, go back to your work on values and vision and what compromises you would have to make in the near and long term, and ask yourself if you can really live with them or if you need to consider another path. Moving on is a bigger decision in this case and should be well considered, but it might be just the moment of clarity you need.

Also, research shows that "people who have rejected an initial request for help are more likely to help the second time around,"[40] so don't count them out completely. That said, know when to move on. Remember that the word no is a complete sentence, and the person owes you no more than that as an explanation.

CHAPTER 10

Additional Strategies to Consider

In my experience, truth and authenticity trump technique every time, but there are some simple strategies that neuroscience has shown us can be very effective in building connections with others. These are the icing on the cake, after you have learned to make your powerful requests.

1. Using the word "together"

The first strategy is using the word "together." "Simply saying the word 'together' can have powerful motivational effects."[41] Dr. Heidi Grant cites research from Priyanka Carr and Greg Walton of Stanford, who found that study participants worked "48 percent longer, solved more problems correctly, and had better recall for what they had seen"[42] when told they were working "together" on puzzles with others even though they would be in separate rooms. Participants also reported finding their work more interesting and persisted longer when they felt this connection.

That's quite a bit of power in one word, but it confirms our strong human need for belonging. "Together" triggers our need for connectedness, engenders trust, and confirms that we are both working toward the same goal.

2. Using phrases that point out shared goals

The second strategy is to use phrases that explicitly link the two of you to wanting the same result. Words such as "we share," "we are both," "I am," "are also," "together we," etc.

- "We share a (concern, idea, passion, etc.)"
  - o I noted from your comments in the meeting that we share a concern for improving our students' learning experience.

- "You and I are ..."
  - o You and I are both from the Midwest and understand how important community is.

- "I am also ..."
  - o I am also a graduate of the state college.

- "We are both ..."
  - o I believe we are both eager to improve communication and collaboration across our business functions.

Highlighting the goals and experiences you share with another person validates their experiences, perceptions, thoughts or ideas that strengthen the in-team or in-group bond and creates an opening for shared opportunity.

Caution: don't make assumptions here by putting words in their mouth or presuming you have a shared goal. Be sure your assertion about the connection you have is on solid ground so as not to lose credibility.

3. Yes, and ...

One of the most powerful tools in conversation is the concept of "Yes, and." This can be a highly useful tool when asking others for support and negotiating to a win-win position. By saying yes, even when the response we get is not exactly what we wanted, we accept the reality created by our partners and begin the collaborative process.[43] The "yes" part means we are fully accepting of the other person's perspective regardless of our own desires and perspectives. The "and" allows us to build on that offer or idea with additional information from our perspective without rejecting or judging the other person's perspective.

If we ask our boss to fund a master's program and they say that they can only support one course this semester, the "Yes, and..." dialogue may look something like this.

You: "I feel an MBA would greatly improve my effectiveness in my new financial management position. I know the company has a program for supporting graduate programs and I request that you provide me with funding to pursue this degree."

Your boss: "Our budget does not support an MBA program at this time, but I could give you funds for one course this semester. Would that help?"

You: "<u>Yes</u>, I appreciate the support, <u>and</u> I would like to get your commitment for a minimum of one course next semester also so I can get both financial course requirements completed before next year's annual report is due. This way I can use that knowledge to continue to improve my input to the annual report."

You have done three things in this response. First, you have shown gratitude. Showing gratitude not only acknowledges and shows appreciation for the offer made by the person, it helps build trust and sustain relationships. It also helps energize the situation and fuels creativity. Second, you have given your boss a reason to continue to support you because you have shown a connection to the work she has assigned you to do in the near term. Third, you have left the door open for an ongoing conversation about your boss's continued support for your graduate learning. It will be no surprise to your boss that you will be making ongoing requests. Also, when your boss creates her next training budget, she will be aware of your need and be more likely to include further funding for you in that plan.

> Saying "yes" has a much different psychological effect than saying "no."
> "If I were to put you into an fMRI scanner and flash the word 'NO' for less than one second, you'd see a sudden release of dozens of stress-producing hormones and neurotransmitters. These chemicals impair logic, reason, language processing, and communication."[44] They also increase irritability, undermine cooperation, and thus inhibit your ability to get the support you need.

From childhood we learn that the word "yes" is used to encourage and continue. In contrast to "no," "yes" produces positive signals in the brain and motivation to initiate approach, or moving toward, behavior.[45] When we help someone to move toward our position by respecting their position, they are more likely to agree to support our request.

Pause

I strongly encourage getting in the habit of replacing the word "but" with the phrase "yes and ..." This small shift can have a remarkable effect on not only getting you more support, but in enabling you to stay open and creative no matter what opposition comes your way.

Moving Forward to Adding New Strategies

1. Using "together" and pointing out shared goals

This exercise prepares you to think about why you have chosen to ask this person for help, and helps you identify the alignment you share. Think of people you want to approach and how you would complete one or more of the sentences below.

- Together we can:

- Together we might:

- We share a concern for:

- You and I are both:

- I am also:

- We are both:

---

2. Yes, and ...

This is a truly wonderful tool that forces you to look for connections supporting both parties by building on each other's insights, awareness, and ideas. Your task here is to identify two or three people who are close to you and teach them the *Yes, and* concept and then practice it together in everyday conversations. Make a game of it and see how long you can build on each other's ideas.

Location	Partners
Home	
Work	
Other	

CHAPTER 11

***

The End of Mind Reading

Let's put mind reading to bed once and for all and focus on making crystal clear requests. In this chapter we will look at a technique to resolve issues where someone's behavior is having an adverse impact on us, or if you are a leader, on the group. In this case we are requesting that the person stop what they are doing and respond in a way that is more effective. There are several variations of this model, but the one I am describing below focuses on one-on-one conversations, preferably held in private when possible.

Often what we need most to achieve our goals or to get unstuck is for someone to do something different. As I mentioned before, our responses—what people say and do—can be habit, mostly unconscious, and not intended to harm us, so we again start with assuming positive intent and then use neutral (descriptive) language. This feedback approach is helpful with people we know but can be used with anyone.

ADIRA

ADIRA is an acronym to help you remember the five steps of this feedback method. It stands for Ask, Describe, Impact, Redirect, Ask. I like that the name Adira means strong and powerful, because it sometimes feels like we need a bit of courage to provide feedback to others.

Leaders often dread giving feedback because they have an old story that feedback is negative, that the person will take it badly, or that it could negatively affect their relationship with the individual. I am hoping by this point that you have shifted to assuming positive intent not just for others, but in yourself. If you honestly care about the individual who is doing something that is causing them to be seen in a negative light, your feedback can be invaluable and save them many weeks or years struggling to understand why they are not advancing as they hoped. When people know you genuinely care about them, they will be much more open to what you have to say. If you're faking it, they will know that too.

A (Ask) Ask if the other person has a minute to talk about something that is important to you.
D (Describe) Describe the behavior you see.
I (Impact) Describe the impact of the behavior.
R (Redirect) Redirect the ineffective behavior.
A (Ask) Ask for a verbal commitment.

Let's go back to the situation with our colleague Henry who always arrives at your meetings after the published start time.

A — <u>Ask</u>: Ask if the other person has a minute to talk about something that is important to you.

The first step of this process involves getting the person alone and letting them know you would like to discuss something important. Letting them know this is important to you puts the other person on notice, and that's good, because it helps them prepare for the conversation. Hopefully, it also helps them be prepared to listen more deeply. In this case you might decide to talk to Henry either before or after the meeting and say, "*Henry, do you have a minute to talk about something that is important to me.*"

If Henry is tight for time, schedule a time to talk at a later date. You have waited this long to address the issue with him, so be sure you set up the right environment for the discussion.

D—Describe: Describe the behavior you see

In this step you describe what you observe in neutral, behavioral terms. In this situation it would be: "*Henry, you have arrived ten minutes after our published meeting start time the last three weeks.*" You are using descriptive language and data so that the only thing that gets addressed is Henry's behavior, not what he is thinking or his intention, because until he reveals his intentions or thoughts, you are only mind reading.

Because your approach is just descriptive, it is much easier for Henry to stay open to discussing the data. Was it actually six or ten minutes after the published meeting start time? Starting from a point of shared agreement about the data creates engagement and an opening toward understanding and the development of a potential solution.

I need to reinforce that just stating what you observe is only the beginning of the process. One of the most frequent mistakes I have seen people make is believing that once they state the problem, it will go away. This assumes:

- The other person acknowledges their behavior—they see and hear what you see and hear (remember the *Crucial Conversations* model);
- They understand the extent of their behavior—the impact it is having on others;
- They know how to fix the problem—that they are capable of identifying a solution that will eliminate the negative impact; and,

- They are committed to making a change.

To get to a point where someone can successfully shift their behavior, we need a few more steps.

I—<u>Impact</u>: Describe the impact of the behavior

The next step involves explaining how the person's current behavior is impacting you, others, the process, or the potential desired outcome. In this case your concern is that Henry has arrived after the published start time the last three weeks.

There are any number of reasons Henry may be late. He may be used to a different culture where start times imply an opportunity for people to get caught up, and the "real" meeting doesn't start until later. He may have a standing meeting just before yours with a higher-level executive whose meetings always run late. He may be very bad at time management. Or, he may not realize how important you consider his input. Until you give Henry the information on the impact his behavior is having, he will not have the information he needs to understand why his attendance at the start of the meeting is considered important. Describing the impact to Henry could sound like:

The behavior: *"Henry, you arrived ten minutes after our published start time the last three weeks."*

The impact: *"I am concerned that we are missing out on your input to key decisions that get discussed before you arrive, and that could have a negative impact on the project."*

R—<u>Redirect</u>: Redirect the ineffective behavior

So now that Henry knows exactly what he is doing that is not working and knows why his being there at the start of the meeting is important, the next step is to help him successfully change his behavior by telling him what you need him to do instead. This is another area where you do not want to have someone struggle to read your mind, but you also want to be open to letting Henry figure out his own solution. In this case you might say:

Redirect the behavior: "*I request you arrive at the published start time for these meetings.*"

Remember how important self-sufficiency can be to many individuals. If you know Henry is much more effective when he gets a say in how he operates, you might choose to ask for his thoughts before offering a solution, such as: "*What could you do to ensure that you arrive at the published start time?*"

What do you mean by "on time"?

The reason I use the term "published start time" in the example above is that the term "on time" is one of the most misunderstood concepts in people's personal and professional lives and one that constantly causes conflict. The concept of being "on time" is different depending on national or organizational culture, so we need to be specific as to what "on time" means to us or to our organization.

Being "on time" may seem like a routine matter and that everyone should understand what it means, but not taking meetings seriously, arriving late, or leaving early is a common frustration in personal and professional relationships alike.

My husband and I both had family situations growing up where one of the family members was constantly late, so we made it a priority to always be on time. In most instances we met each other's expectations and had few problems, except when it came to leaving the house at a certain time after we moved. We were both very busy during this time, trying to squeeze every opportunity out of our days, and constantly found that we were late and blaming each other.

Neither of us understood why we were finding ourselves late but knew it was becoming a problem. Then one evening when we were scheduled to leave for a dinner party, I went to look for Steve and noticed he was still on the computer. Thinking I had a few minutes, I put a *quick* load of laundry in the washing machine. While I was putting the laundry in, Steve looked for me and, seeing I was still busy, went back on his computer to do one *quick* thing. When we found ourselves late, of course, I blamed him and he blamed me.

We all do this. Just one more thing that will just take a second, and we are late. When this gets compounded with multiple people, you see the situation Steve and I found ourselves in. We decided at this point to adopt the concept we called "target time." We decided when one of us said *"target time"* that it meant stop whatever you are doing to ensure you are ready to walk out the door at that exact time. Without actually saying it, we also began to understand that *"target time"* also meant we were making a verbal commitment of respect to each other.

Ingrid Bens, one of the most well-known and skilled master facilitators, uses an eight-step model when facilitating groups. I have adopted three steps from her model because I have found this language to be especially powerful when behaviors threaten both effectiveness and relationships:[46]

1. Describe the behavior you see. *I am noticing that …*
2. Describe the impact. *I am concerned that …*
3. Redirect the ineffective behavior. *"I request you"* (define the action you want instead) or *"What could, or What will, you do"* (to ensure that a specific action takes place).[47]

I have changed this third step from Ingrid's phrase of "I need you to …" to use the word "request" because I have found it adds clarity. It also provides autonomy for the other person to come up with his or her own solutions.

A—<u>Ask</u>: Ask for a verbal commitment

In addition, I have added a final step to this formula, that of requiring a verbal commitment by the person to change their behavior. In this case it would be: *"Do I have your commitment to arrive at the published start time for these meetings in the future?"*

The key is to be sure to wait for the person to actually reply and not just move on before they have had a chance to speak, even when you may feel that potentially awkward period of silence. This silence could be useful. It may be giving the person the time they need to either understand the importance of changing their behavior or to think of an alternative solution that may work better.

A verbal commitment is a public declaration to act. According to *Psychology Today*, "People who make verbal commitments feel obligated to follow through on their commitments or risk cognitive dissonance or social rejection."[48] It is much more difficult for someone to neglect a stated commitment than one that is implied. As we discussed before, the reason for this is that we feel mental discomfort when we try to hold two contradictory beliefs or ideas in our mind simultaneously. Acting against what we said we would do sets up this conflict. And, because our brains crave psychological consistency in order to function well in the real world, we work to resolve this conflict by behaving in the way we committed to behave. When a psychologically healthy person acts in a way that is inconsistent with how they have declared they will act, they are highly motivated to resolve this inconsistency.

There is another, sometimes stronger, force that drives us to meet our stated commitments: the fear of social rejection. Not meeting our commitments threatens our status with our tribe or community and evokes all those threats associated with being ostracized socially.

Be aware of qualifiers when you get the person's response. Responses such as "I'll try" or "If I can" are *not* commitments. If you get this qualified response, you can pretty much be sure the person's behavior will not change. In this case, you need to go further and ask the question "*What could you do in order to ensure that …?*" or "*What will it take for you to …?*" Again, if you are dealing with someone who has high control or autonomy needs, they may need to come up with their own solution, and that's fine. As long as you get the behavior change needed.

For the Henry example, these four steps would be:

1. "Henry, I notice that you have arrived ten minutes later than the published start time for our meeting the last three weeks."
2. "I am concerned that we are missing out on your input to some key decisions that get discussed before you arrive."
3. "I request you arrive at the published meeting start time." Or, "What could you do to ensure you can be here for the entire meeting?"
4. "Do I have your commitment to arrive at the published start time for these meetings in the future?"

As we discussed, using labels and making negative attributions are not easy habits to break. Why? Because with the old way, *we get to be right or make others wrong.* It is also easier because we don't have to figure out just what the person is doing that is bothering us. That requires the hard work of observing and thinking versus just going with our own emotional reaction.

Stopping your brain from judgment when it becomes triggered by someone else's behavior is a practice that takes time. When someone's actions or words make you uneasy or angry, you can use the "I wonder why" question. *"I wonder why Henry arriving late bothers me so much?"* This will help you be more observant in the moment as to exactly what is affecting you.

Below is a list of common situations that could require you to confront someone's behavior. Continue to notice the connections with the SCARF model when your threat response is triggered.

- ➤ Challenging your role, your authority, your intelligence, your opinion, or anything else. (Status)
- ➤ Being micromanaged or told what to do. (Autonomy)
- ➤ Being given a negative facial expression or rolling of eyes. (Status/Relatedness)
- ➤ Using inappropriate humor, sarcasm, or cynicism. (Status)
- ➤ Dominating a conversation or being talked over. (Autonomy/Status)
- ➤ Not responding to you, being ignored. (Relatedness)
- ➤ Being treated differently than you see others being treated. (Fairness)

The most important aspect of this tool is that it helps build relationships, and those relationships are the key to getting the support you need from others. So, let's go back to the scenario where Dan quickly entered his office.

1. "Dan, I noticed you quickly enter your office when I was approaching."
2. "I am concerned that you may be angry with me."
3. "I want to be sure that we continue to have a good working relationship and would appreciate it if you would take a minute to acknowledge me when we meet or let me know if you are angry so we can resolve any problems."
4. "Do I have your commitment to make this acknowledgment in the future?" Or "Would you be willing to do that?"

I know it can sound awkward in some cultures to ask for a commitment, so just try it out and use your own words.

With practice, describing what someone does in behavioral terms not only gets easier, it also gives us the pause we need to think clearly and respond in a more effective way. Let's look at a few more common examples of how we can move from judgment and attribution to describing words and behaviors.

From Judgment or Attribution	To Words and Behaviors
She is trying to shut me down.	She started speaking before I had finished making my point.
He is disrespectful and a creep.	He looked at my body instead of looking me in the eye when we were talking.
She was trying to seduce me.	She rubbed my back.
He is so sensitive.	When I said he looked nice today, he gave me a concerned look and walked away.
She's always late. She thinks she is more important than the rest of us.	She arrived ten minutes after the meeting start time on Tuesday and twelve minutes after the start time today.
He doesn't like working with women.	When he is the only man in the meeting, he leaves right after he delivers his report.

Watch your language!

"Watch your language" is an idiom that means to pay attention to what you are saying. As I said before, much of what we say is by habit and likely unconscious, so it is important to be aware of our choice of words and how they may be impacting our outcomes. By using negative words like "She's a pain" or minimalizing qualifiers such as "I'm *just* an assistant" on yourself or others, you set them and yourself up for failure. Just the opposite happens when you use positive words.

Describe behaviors in neutral terms as much as possible. In the example of our co-worker Dan above, instead of, "*I saw a co-worker down the hall, and as I approached him, he <u>ducked</u> into someone's office,*" a neutral way of saying this would be, "*I saw a co-worker down the hall, and as I approached him, he <u>turned</u> into someone's office.*" One word can make all the difference in how you interpret their actions and whether you get triggered. What are the chances we are going to ask the person who *ducked* for something we need from them?

The bottom line is we believe the stories we tell ourselves. When we tell ourselves the answer is "no" before we ask the question, we've stopped our growth and our path to success.[49]

The story we tell ourselves always determines the actions we are willing to take.

So, what new strategies can we use when our old stories hold us back from making a request to get what we need? Our brains will take the path of least resistance, which is our old story line that usually holds us back. Because we tend to fall back into our default response, it is important to have a new strategy that will overcome this habit—think If-Then.

Moving Forward to End Mind Reading

A—<u>Ask</u>: Ask if the other person has a minute to talk about something that is important to you.

- Does the opportunity to have a one-on-one conversation exist?
- Is this the right time to have this conversation?
- When would be a better time?

D—<u>Describe</u>: Describe the behavior you see.

- What is this person doing that is having a negative impact on you, the group, or the organization?
- Ask the "I wonder why" question.

I—<u>Impact</u>: Describe the impact of the behavior.

- Why is this an issue?
- Is what they are doing just another approach you don't agree with or is it really having a negative impact on you, your relationship, or the group?

R—<u>Redirect</u>: Redirect the ineffective behavior.

- What would you like them to do instead?
- Are they someone who would prefer to identify their own strategy to deal with the issue?

A—<u>Ask</u>: Ask for a verbal commitment.

- Did you remember to ask for a verbal commitment?
- Did they make one, equivocate, or refuse?

Stage 4: If You Don't Ask, the Answer Is Always No

EPILOGUE

I hope you enjoyed *If You Don't Ask, the Answer Is Always No*. Because everyone has their own learning style, I hope that this information and workbook approach of *If You Don't Ask, the Answer Is Always No* was helpful to you. But this is not your only learning option. Other learning offerings include:

❑ *If You Don't Ask, the Answer Is Always No* **Online:** If you prefer learning with others or via a more instructional approach, this option takes you through the material and exercises in a more structured way.

❑ *If You Don't Ask, the Answer Is Always No* **for Organizations:** This in-person course gives leaders an opportunity to learn together and develop a common framework for supporting each other's leader within their organization.

❑ *If You Don't Ask, the Answer Is Always No* **Coaching:** Our one-on-one coaching, for those who prefer a more individual approach.

More information is available at my website:

Christinerwilliams.com

Epilogue

ENDNOTES

1   Julie Beck, "Life's Stories: How you arrange the plot points of your life into a narrative can shape who you are—and is a fundamental part of being human," *The Atlantic*, August 10, 2015, https://www.theatlantic.com/health/archive/2015/08/life-stories-narrative-psychology-redemption-mental-health/400796/

2   Kerry Patterson, Joseph Grenny, Ron McMillan, and Al Switzler, *Crucial Conversations* (New York: McGraw-Hill, 2012), 109.

3   Patterson et al., *Crucial Conversations*, 109.

4   Martin Luenendonk, "How to Collaborate with and Influence People Using the SCARF Model," *CLEVERism* (website), August 3, 2016, https://www.cleverism.com/scarf-model-influence-people/

5   Wikipedia, "Shunning," last modified May 30, 2021, https://en.wikipedia.org/wiki/Shunning

6   Wikipedia, "In-group and out-group," last modified May 12, 2021, https://en.wikipedia.org/wiki/Ingroup_and_outgroup

7   Elliot Aronson, Timothy D. Wilson, Robin M. Akert, and Samuel R. Sommers, *Social Psychology*, 9th ed. (London: Pearson Education, 2015).

8   Katherine Harmon, "Social Ties Boost Survival by 50 Percent," *Scientific American*, July 28, 2010, https://www.scientificamerican.com/article/relationships-boost-survival/

9   Mel Schwartz, "Why Is It So Important to Be Right?" *Psychology Today*, March 7, 2011, https://www.psychologytoday.com/blog/shift-mind/201103/why-is-it-so-important-be-right

10 Alex Lickerman, "What Do You Want?" *Psychology Today*, August 5, 2012, https://www.psychologytoday.com/us/blog/happiness-in-world/201208/what-do-you-want

11 Lickerman, "What Do You Want?"

12 Vivian Lawry, "Psychology of Uncertainty: Better the Devil You Know," vivianlawry.com, July 9, 2015, http://vivianlawry.com/psychology-of-uncertainty-better-the-devil-you-know/

13 Alex Lickerman, "The Desire for Autonomy," *Psychology Today*, May 6, 2012, https://www.psychologytoday.com/blog/happiness-in-world/201205/the-desire-autonomy

14 David Rock, *Your Brain at Work* (New York: HarperCollins, 2009), 123.

15 Netta Weinstein, Nicole Legate, William S. Ryan, and Laura Hemmy, "Autonomous orientation predicts longevity: New findings from the Nun Study," *Journal of Personality* 87, no. 2 (2019): 181–193, https://doi.org/10.1111/jopy.12379. Choiceful behavior was only one of the predictors of longevity.

16 Blossom Yen-Ju Lin, Yung-Kai Lin, Cheng-Chieh Lin, and Tien-Tse Lin, "Job autonomy, its predisposition and its relation to work outcomes in community health centers in Taiwan," *Health Promotional International* 28, no. 2 (June 2013): 166–177, https://doi.org/10.1093/heapro/dar091

17 Simon Moesgaard, "The Three Most Basic Psychological Needs, and Why We Need to Satisfy Them," reflectd.com, March 19, 2015, http://reflectd.co/2015/03/19/the-three-most-basic-psychological-needs-and-why-we-need-to-satisfy-them/

18 Guy Winch, "Why rejection hurts so much—and what to do about it," ideas.ted.com, December 8, 2015, https://ideas.ted.com/why-rejection-hurts-so-much-and-what-to-do-about-it/

19 Mark A. Whatley, Adele Rhodes, Richard H. Smith, and J. Matthew Webster, "The Effect of a Favor on Public and Private Compliance: How Internalized Is the Norm of Reciprocity?" *Basic and Applied Social Psychology* 21, no. 3 (1999): 251–259.

20 Wikipedia, "Norm of reciprocity," last modified June 1, 2021, https://en.wikipedia.org/wiki/Norm_of_reciprocity

21 Ernst Fehr and Klaus M. Schmidt, "Theories of Fairness and Reciprocity—Evidence and Economic Applications," in Mathias Dewatripont, Lars Peter Hansen and Stephen J. Turnovsky, *Advances in Economics and Econometrics, Economic Society Monographs, Eighth World Congress*, Vol. 1 (2003): 208–257, http://web.mit.edu/14.193/www/WorldCongress-IEW-Version6Oct03.pdf

22 Jane McGrath, "10 Ridiculous Victorian Etiquette Rules," How Stuff Works (website), May 12, 2021, https://people.howstuffworks.com/10-ridiculous-victorian-etiquette-rules.htm

23 Patterson et al., *Crucial Conversations*, 101.

24 Kolyanne Russ, "What Annoys You and What You Hate About Others is Your Own Reflection," *Medium*, January 17, 2018, https://medium.com/@kolyanne/what-annoys-you-and-what-you-hate-about-others-is-your-own-reflection-64c28ecc0032

25 Beverly Blanchard, "The Law of Reflection," blog, April 14, 2013, http://beverlyblanchard.blogspot.com/2013/04/the-law-of-reflection.html

26   Alex Lickerman, "How to Manage Frustration," *Psychology Today*, February 19, 2012, https://www.psychologytoday.com/us/blog/happiness-in-world/201202/how-manage-frustration

27   Gayle Katz, "Name Calling: How Toxic People Use It as An Emotional Weapon, and What You Can Do About It," Grounded Girl's Guide, October 10, 2016, http://www.groundedgirlsguide.com/toxic-people/2016/10/20/name-calling-emotional-weapon/

28   Nick Haslam, "The Psychology of Insults," *The Conversation*, University of Melbourne, January 23, 2017, https://theconversation.com/the-psychology-of-insults-71738

29   Lisa Gaudet, "The Rewards of Assuming Positive Intent," Quickbase blog, May 3, 2011, https://www.quickbase.com/blog/the-rewards-of-assuming-positive-intent

30   Miki Kashtan, "Intention and Effect," *Psychology Today*, August 23, 2013, https://www.psychologytoday.com/blog/acquired-spontaneity/201308/intention-and-effect

31   Karman Akbarzadeh, "Five Essential Elements of Powerful Vision Statements," Dream Achievers Academy blog, https://www.dreamachieversacademy.com/five-elements/

32   "Why is Self-Awareness Important as a Leader?" Level Up Leadership (website), March 6, 2019, http://levelupleadership.com/why-is-self-awareness-important-as-a-leader/

33   *The Autobiography of Benjamin Franklin*, 1791.

34   Wikipedia, "Leadership," last modified July 23, 2021, https://en.wikipedia.org/wiki/Leadership

35   David Rock and Khalil Smith, "How to Be an Ally in This Moment: Listen Deeply, Unite Widely, Act Boldly," *Forbes*, June 3, 2020, https://www.forbes.com/sites/davidrock/2020/06/03/leadership-in-this-moment-listen-deeply-unite-widely-act-boldly/#49473d7a22cd

36   Heidi Grant, *Reinforcements: How to Get People to Help You* (Boston: Harvard Business Review Press, 2018), 159.

37   "Be Part of Something Bigger," Action for Happiness website, https://www.actionforhappiness.org/10-keys-to-happier-living/be-part-of-something-bigger/details

38   Peter Economy, "Steve Jobs on the Remarkable Power of Asking for Help," *Inc.*, June 11, 2015, https://www.inc.com/peter-economy/steve-jobs-on-the-remarkable-power-of-asking-for-what-you-want.html

Endnotes

39 "Get to the Point: The Merits of Being Brief in your Communication," Slide Express website, October 23, 2018, https://www.slidexpress.com/get-to-the-point-the-merits-of-being-brief-in-your-communication/

40 Grant, *Reinforcements*, 29.

41 Grant, *Reinforcements*, 135.

42 Grant, *Reinforcements*, 136.

43 Wikipedia, "Yes, and…" last modified February 12, 2021, https://en.wikipedia.org/wiki/Yes,_and...

44 Andrew Newberg and Mark Waldman, "Why This Word Is So Dangerous to Say or Hear," *Psychology Today*, August 1, 2012, https://www.psychologytoday.com/blog/words-can-change-your-brain/201208/the-most-dangerous-word-in-the-world

45 Nelly Alia-Klein, Rita Z. Goldstein, Dardo Tomasi, Lei Zhang, Stephanie Fagin-Jones, Frank Telang, Gene-Jack Wang, Joanna S. Fowler, and Nora D. Volkow, "What is in a Word? No versus Yes Differently Engage the Lateral Orbitofrontal Cortex," *Emotion* 7, no. 3 (2007): 649–659, https://www.ncbi.nlm.nih.gov/pmc/articles/PMC2443710/

46 Ingrid Bens, *Advanced Facilitation Strategies, Tools and Techniques to Master Difficult Situations* (San Francisco: Jossey-Bass, 2005), 88.

47 I have changed this phrase in Step 3 from "I need you to …" to "I request" and "What should we do …" to "What could, or what will, you do differently …"

48 Jack Schafer, "Get Things Done—Get a Verbal Commitment," *Psychology Today*, December 3, 2012, https://www.psychologytoday.com/blog/let-their-words-do-the-talking/201212/get-things-done-get-verbal-commitment

49 "Change Your Story," Tony Robbins website, https://www.tonyrobbins.com/stories/change-your-story/

ABOUT THE AUTHOR

Chris Williams is a public speaker, consultant, coach, and teacher. She has over thirty years of experience designing and delivering programs and strategies that enable leaders and organizations to improve performance and achieve their goals. For fifteen years, Chris served as director of a number of NASA's most successful agency-wide leadership development programs. Her cutting-edge, award-winning programs are considered world-class in industry and government, and her expertise is sought in areas of leadership development, organizational change, and the application of neuroscience to improving leader and organizational effectiveness. As a result of her research at NASA, she authored a number of articles documenting the leadership and executive behaviors that drive NASA's success.

www.ingramcontent.com/pod-product-compliance
Lightning Source LLC
Chambersburg PA
CBHW072133020426
42334CB00018B/1780